Child
&
Adolescent
Life Stories

In memory of Kathy's parents, Betty and Thomas Voegtle.
In memory of Marguerite's dad, Peter Guadagni.

Child & Adolescent Life Stories

Perspectives From Youth, Parents, and Teachers

Marguerite G. Lodico
Katherine H. Voegtle
The College of Saint Rose

SAGE Publications
Thousand Oaks ▪ London ▪ New Delhi

For information:

Sage Publications, Inc.
2455 Teller Road
Thousand Oaks, California 91320
E-mail: order@sagepub.com

Sage Publications Ltd.
1 Oliver's Yard
55 City Road
London EC1Y 1SP
United Kingdom

Sage Publications India Pvt. Ltd.
B-42, Panchsheel Enclave
Post Box 4109
New Delhi 110 017 India

Printed in the United States of America

Library of Congress Cataloging-in-Publication Data

Lodico, Marguerite G.
Child and adolescent life stories: Perspectives from youth, parents, and teachers / Marguerite G. Lodico and Katherine H. Voegtle.
    p. cm.
Includes bibliographical references and index.
ISBN 1-4129-0562-1 (cloth) — ISBN 1-4129-0563-X (pbk.)
    1. Child development—Case studies. I. Voegtle, Katherine H. II. Title.
HQ769.L614 2005
305.231—dc22

                                    2004022903

This book is printed on acid-free paper.

05 06 07 08 09 10 9 8 7 6 5 4 3 2 1

Acquisitions Editor:	Diane McDaniel
Editorial Assistant:	Marta Peimer
Production Editor:	Laureen Shea
Copy Editor:	Diana Breti
Typesetter:	C&M Digitals (P) Ltd.
Proofreader:	Kevin Gleason
Indexer:	Paul Corrington
Cover Designer:	Janet Foulger

CONTENTS

ACKNOWLEDGMENTS

To paraphrase a wise saying about child development, it takes a whole community to birth a book! Here we would like to thank all of the people who have contributed to the making of this book.

First and most essential were the youth, parents, and teachers who were willing to share their lives with us and discuss some often painful or difficult experiences. It was their willingness to reflect deeply on the people and events in their lives and their ability to communicate their insights in an articulate and moving manner that made this book possible. We have attempted to preserve, as much as possible, the eloquent words that they used to describe their life stories. Their stories were our inspiration to complete this book, and they helped us appreciate even more profoundly the rich complexity of human development.

Our college, The College of Saint Rose, has also been a generous supporter of this project from its inception. The college granted us sabbatical leaves during the same academic year (based on a joint application) to conduct our research and collaborate on writing. Since a book usually has a gestation period of longer than nine months (the academic year) and requires financial commitments, our college also provided professional development grants to support our research and awarded us course reductions during two different semesters to continue our writing and conduct research for the pedagogical sections of the book. One of our strongest supporters has been Crystal Gips, Dean of the School of Education. It is an indication of the commitment that The College of Saint Rose and Dean Gips place on excellent teaching and scholarship that they have supported us so fully throughout this project.

Our three graduate assistants, Maggie Russom, Gina Ciccone, and Elizabeth Gerron, also gave invaluable assistance to us. Maggie's efforts came early on as she cheerfully transcribed many pages of interviews and helped with data analysis. She also made contacts with families and assisted in interviewing. Gina so impressed us with her skill in editing cases that we asked her to conduct interviews and write a case. As anyone who reads her case, "Frank: Confronting Change and Taking a Stand in Middle School," can see, she was a professional in every sense of the word and we owe a huge debt of gratitude to her. Liz's contributions came toward the end of the writing process. She provided valuable assistance in writing discussion questions, collecting Web resources, and editing and formatting the final drafts.

Members of our Department of Educational Psychology have also supported us in many ways. James Allen sparked our initial interest in case studies through his research on teaching with cases and his superb modeling of how cases could be used in teaching. Aviva Bower stimulated our interest in narrative studies and offered her expertise in qualitative research. She also piloted cases in her classes on child and adolescent development and provided editorial suggestions. Other members of our department filled in for us when we were on leave and offered support and creative suggestions to us as we worked. Our department chairs, Ismael Ramos and Richard Brody, graciously found replacements to teach our courses.

While everyone suffers a bit from evaluation anxiety, we have nothing but gratitude for the reviewers who provided extensive comments and suggestions after reading our prospectus and drafts of our cases. Specifically, we would like to express our thanks to Karen M. Dutt-Doner at Niagara University, M. Randal Spaid at Mercer University, and anonymous reviewers at William Patterson University and Texas A&M University, Kingsville, for reviewing our prospectus. Thanks are also due to Miles Anthony Irving at Georgia State University; Judith Rhoden at the University of North Carolina, Charlotte; Linda R. Kroll at Mills College; Deanna Nekovei at Texas A&M University, Kingsville; and Karen M. Dutt-Doner at Niagara University for reviewing the drafts of the cases. Our reviewers certainly helped us develop our ideas about the book and helped make the cases more readable and useful as teaching tools.

It has also been a pleasure to work with Diane McDaniel, our editor at Sage, and the members of Sage's editorial and production staff. Diane was so positive and encouraging at the start that she helped us believe in ourselves. She gently urged us on at each stage of the project and seemed to understand when we needed additional time or support. Her facilitation of the review process greatly simplified our job. Marta Peimer, our editorial assistant, eased the transition from writing to production and kept us well organized. They have made the overwhelming task of writing a book seem doable.

Finally, we would like to thank our families and significant others for their emotional support and creative input. Kathy's brother, Tom, made invaluable contacts for us with school districts and families and educated us about the joys and perils of urban education. Kathy's partner, Jim, made many meals, listened to endless diatribes about inflexible schools, provided needed comic relief, and read and edited cases with the precision and astuteness that so endear this well-read philosopher to her. Marguerite's husband, Phil, supported her throughout this entire project. With his clear and focused legal mind, he gently critiqued the logic and flow of each case. Marguerite's two children, Philip and Andrea, provided constant encouragement and always believed that this book would be a reality.

INTRODUCTION

———•◦•———

USING CASES TO UNDERSTAND
HUMAN DEVELOPMENT

How many times can you recall a child saying to you, "Tell me a story"? Children understand that stories are fun ways to learn about the world around them. Developmental researchers are also beginning to appreciate the power of stories in teaching about children and adolescents, although they often use more sophisticated terms, such as case studies, autobiographies, life stories, or narratives, to describe their stories. A growing number of researchers are looking to qualitative methods as ways of both studying and teaching about human development (Bruner, 1990; Corcoran, 1996; Jessor & Colby, 1996; Mayo, 2002; Vitz, 1990). In part, this reflects dissatisfaction with the overly quantitative methods frequently used to study development. Mishler (1996) has argued that developmental research that primarily studies variables in large populations has lost sight of the individual person and the importance of unique "deviations" from general patterns by individuals. Bruner (1990) has described how he began his professional life as a developmental researcher using mostly quantitative methods, but gradually came to value stories or narratives as a "mode of knowing" used by children to understand their own lives and to find their place within their culture. More recent researchers have used ethnographic methods, including interviews, observations, and narrative analysis, to more fully represent the experiences of youth and their perspectives on a wide variety of social issues (Carger, 1996; Fine & Weiss, 2003; Kozol, 2000).

This book was written to help persons taking or teaching courses in human development reassert the importance of studying and understanding individual children and their stories by using qualitative methods, specifically case studies, as teaching and learning tools. Case studies have a long history as *research* methods in studying human development (e.g., Erikson, 1968; Freud, 1963; Maslow, 1970), although the use of cases to *teach* about development is a more recent trend. When we started to use cases in teaching about development, we struggled with the question of what type of cases could help students understand the full context of children's lives, including the influences of family, community, and culture. As professors of educational psychology, we wanted students to think about the complex array of factors that influence development over the course of a child's or adolescent's life. Development is a complicated process that occurs within a large social context. In order to fully understand that social context and its influence on development, we felt that students needed to consider perspectives from the youth themselves as well as other significant individuals in their social setting. Available cases were typically written only from one perspective (the youth or a teacher) or were very brief with little background or contextual information.

Therefore, we decided to write case studies of children and adolescents from a variety of settings and backgrounds that included the perspectives of the youth, their parents, and their teachers. In this book, these different perspectives, which may or may not be in agreement, give you an opportunity to see and analyze development using a variety of windows. The cases presented in this book are all life histories, in that they include information from all parts of the youths' lives. Some of the cases are detailed portraits of many events and relationships in the youth's life and others are briefer accounts of a few critical incidents and relationships with just enough contextual information to understand these particulars. For clarity and to avoid unnecessarily creating new jargon, we have used the term "case study" to apply to all of the stories in this book.

This introduction will describe how these case studies were developed and how they can be used in classes on human development. In addition, it will identify the organizational aids included in this book and suggest strategies for reading and analyzing cases in human development courses.

How the Case Studies Were Developed

As noted above, our initial goal in writing this book was to develop case studies of children with diverse backgrounds who represented the full range of ages covered in courses on child and adolescent development. The youth and families were selected based on referrals from teachers and colleagues who worked closely with families in a variety of settings. We used a criterion-based purposive sampling method, asking our contacts to identify families with children and parents from different family structures and sociocultural backgrounds who would be willing to talk about their personal histories. As we completed each case study, we looked for families who were different in some way from the ones we had completed (e.g., based on the child's age, gender, family background, or personal challenges faced by the youth).

Another consideration was that the cases would allow discussion of many of the issues included in these development courses, such as nature versus nurture, teenage pregnancy, death of a loved one, academic difficulties, self-esteem, living with a disability, establishing peer relationships, finding one's identity, parenting styles, child abuse, and domestic violence.

We met with each youth and parent to talk about the nature and goals of the project. Specifically, they were told that we had three goals: (1) to create stories or case studies about the lives of children and teenagers in the United States today, (2) to produce a book containing these stories that would be used by students who were studying about children or preparing to become classroom teachers, and (3) to use this book to help these students understand what is important in the lives of children and teenagers. The potential participants were told that they would have a chance to review and make corrections to transcripts of their interviews and give their approval for us to use this information in the final case study write-up. For the younger children, transcript and case study reviews were done by the parent. In the final case studies, names of the participants and the name and location of the school at which the observations occurred were changed to maintain confidentiality. However, all of the cases depict real youth in real-world settings.

For each case study, semi-structured interviews were conducted with a youth, parent, and teacher in order to obtain a variety of perspectives. The locations and times of the interviews were set up to be convenient and comfortable for the participants. At least two interviews were conducted with the youth, and typically one with the teacher and the parent or guardian. Informal conversations with youth, teachers, and parents or guardians provided additional information summarized in field notes, which was sometimes used in the cases. The cases included youth from urban, suburban, and rural areas in midwestern, northeastern, and southeastern states. We developed a set of broad questions that were posed to all youth (the language was adapted to be appropriate to the age of the youth), asking them to tell us about significant relationships that they had formed with others and the events and activities in their lives that they felt were important. The questions focused on specifics about each child's life, including the child's interests, activities, goals, relationships with others, school and academic experiences, happy and sad times, and other issues, events, or problems. A similar set of questions was designed for their parents and teachers to provide multiple perspectives on similar issues and events. In all interviews, the questions formed a starting point for discussion and the participants were encouraged to talk freely about whatever they felt was significant in their lives. Participants were told that they had the right to decline to answer any question and withdraw from the project at any time. While no participants declined to participate, many youth did redirect the course of the interview by focusing on particular events and relationships that had a powerful impact on them. At the end of each interview, participants were invited to share anything that they felt was important that had not been discussed in the interview and were then asked to highlight the things that they felt absolutely had to be included in their case study. The interviews were tape-recorded and then transcribed for analysis. A series of naturalistic observations, using both participant and nonparticipant approaches, were conducted by accompanying the youth to events in school or community settings or simply observing classroom or community activities in which the youth participated. The observations were set up in consultation with the youth, their parents or guardians, and teachers. The number and length of the observations varied with the youth. Sometimes we accompanied a youth to a favorite place or event. In other observations, we sat in on classes, concerts, or other events at the youth's school.

We collected our data during sequential sabbatical leaves from teaching in which one of us was intensely involved in interviewing and observation while the other served as a peer debriefer. Data were analyzed as we collected it, and initial themes and issues were identified first by the person who collected the data. The peer debriefer also reviewed transcripts and field notes to check on the credibility of the analysis. We selected events, themes, and quotes to highlight in each case based on two criteria: (1) Did the selection accurately represent the life of the youth from one or more perspectives, and (2) Would the selection allow analysis of issues relevant to the study of child and adolescent development? All youth and their parents had a chance to review the final cases. We then piloted the cases in undergraduate and graduate classes in Child and Adolescent Development and in some graduate courses in Educational Psychology. Based on feedback from our students, colleagues who used the cases in their classes, and our own observations, we added contextual and background information and rewrote sections of the cases to facilitate analysis and clarify sections of the cases.

Organization of the Book

Each case study in this book tells the youth's life story, including the events and relationships that have influenced the child or adolescent and his or her physical, cognitive, social, and emotional development. The case studies are organized chronologically according to the age of the youth at the time of the interview. The cases range from early childhood (the youngest child was four years old) through late adolescence (the oldest youth was 18 years old). Since each case study is a life history, however, it may cover events and issues from multiple ages. As noted earlier, cases also vary in length. Some cases depict many events over the course of the child's or adolescent's life in detail, while others focus on a couple of key events or relationships. This variety provides more flexibility in how the cases can be used. Brief cases are good starting points for the process of case analysis or for illustrating selected concepts without the complexity of a full life history. Longer case studies are useful in thinking about ways to apply broader theories of development or how different aspects of development (e.g., cognitive, social, emotional, moral) might be interrelated.

Each case begins with a bulleted list of Primary and Secondary Issues addressed in the case. Don't expect all of the terms to be included in the case. These are issues that most likely are addressed in developmental courses, and they can serve as advance organizers to help you begin to identify the important information presented in the case. At the end of each case are Discussion Questions, Applying Theoretical Perspectives Questions, Class Activities, and Research Suggestions. The questions and activities may also help you to decide what information from the case to highlight or record, while the research suggestions provide ideas for further study. One of the values of teaching with case studies is that they allow you to explore topics that are not covered in detail in most textbooks (e.g., family alcoholism). To help you make sense of these "extra" topics, we have included Readings and Resources for additional research at the end of each case. These Readings and Resources may be assigned prior to reading the case or incorporated into class presentations.

Textbooks and courses in human development typically take either an age-graded or topical approach. A Chart of Cases organized chronologically by the age of the child and summarizing background information and issues for each case is included at the end of this introduction. It can be used to get an overview of the cases before reading them and to decide which ones you want to read or include in the course. If your course takes an age-graded approach, we suggest that you analyze cases based on the age of the child at the end of the unit covering that age period. This allows you to consider multiple aspects of development and examine how the different areas of development are interconnected. If your course takes a topical approach, the Chart of Cases can help to see which cases cover issues addressed by each topic. Since most cases include issues typically covered by several chapters of a topical developmental text, the cases can also help you review information from earlier chapters or integrate information across chapters. Since these case studies are based on real-life histories, they are often messy (e.g., they include many complex issues) and do not match up completely with the organization or content of developmental textbooks. We have found that one advantage of the holistic nature of case studies is they allow you to build on earlier learning and develop a more complete picture of the whole child.

Additionally, following the Chart of Cases you will find a set of Connecting Across Cases questions (questions that include issues addressed in several cases) designed to encourage students to think about how certain issues influence youth in different ways. Some of these questions identify specific cases for analysis and others allow you to select cases for discussion. When the Connecting Across Cases questions are tied to specific cases, the questions are also referenced after the Applying Theoretical Perspective section in the case.

Strategies for Analyzing Cases

Research on using cases in courses in educational psychology, teacher education, and special education has expanded so rapidly in the last 25 years that it has its own descriptor, "case method," in electronic databases. Some of the methods used to teach with case studies identified in past research are clearly applicable in human development. This section will summarize some general strategies for analyzing case studies based on the extensive research on the use of the case method as a teaching and learning approach in education (Allen, 1995; Block, 1996; Kleinfeld, 1991; Merseth, 1991, 1994; Mostert & Kauffman, 1992; Semrau & Fitzgerald, 1995; Shulman, 1992; Sudzina, 1997; Sykes & Bird, 1993–1994; Wasserman, 1994). More specific strategies for using the cases in this book in human development courses will also be discussed.

• Cases can be used to either illustrate or apply theories, research, or principles of development. Cases are an effective way to help deepen your understanding of theories of development. We usually have our students apply two different theories to the same case. This helps them understand how the theories emphasize different aspects of development. The case helps students understand the often abstract concepts presented by theories, such as ecological theory. In a case such as "Jaime: Crossing Cultures and Celebrating Life," the theory reminds students to examine all of the social systems in Jaime's life, including macrosystem influences such as immigration laws and cultural differences. Each case in this book presents discussion questions that highlight one or more theories or concepts that could be applied to the case. An alternative approach is to simply generate a list of concepts and discuss how these might be applied to the case. For example, concepts that could be applied to "Frank: Confronting Change and Taking a Stand" include empathy, moral reasoning, depression, peer status, cliques, rural versus suburban communities, and parent involvement.

• Small groups or large groups can discuss issues involved in the case and possible approaches or interventions that could be taken with the youth. For example, "Ben: Having His Way at Preschool and Home" provides a very useful framework for discussion of differences in discipline between home and school as well as building of family-school partnerships. "Nicole and Brooke: Homeschooled Fraternal Twins" can be used to discuss the pros and cons of homeschooling and issues of nature versus nurture in relation to the twins.

• Cases can be used to develop plans for assessment, instruction, or intervention. Again, the case "Ben: Having His Way at Preschool and Home" can be used to discuss how we assess social skills in children. "Beth: Finding

Her Strengths" presents a case in which questions could be raised about assessment for a learning disability. "Emily's World" presents a child with autism, and students could discuss how the sensitive instruction of teachers and active advocacy of her mother promoted high levels of development.

- Cases can be used to prepare for field experiences by presenting scenarios that might be encountered in the field. Alternatively, cases can enrich field experiences by presenting diverse settings or issues not present in the field experience. For example, one of our colleagues used the case on Ben after her class had observed at a preschool center. It helped to identify the types of conflicts that might not be apparent after only one day of observations and provided a possible parent's perspective on a preschool program as well.

- For some cases, you might want to role-play conversations for situations described in the case as a way of refining social and communication skills so important to teachers. For example, in "Hector: Talking Through Troubles," a teacher talks with a student about the murder of one of his friends. As part of our discussion of helping children cope with death and loss, we have our students create a role play of the conversation that might occur.

- Cases can be used as a means of assessment of your understanding of course content through written analyses, case competitions, exam questions, or group or team discussions. We have used our cases as the basis for essay questions that require students to integrate information across multiple areas or ages. The questions for discussion at the end of each case may be used as a basis for class discussion or as the basis for written papers or essay questions. Students might be assigned all questions as homework, or different questions may be assigned to individuals in a group in a jigsaw type of activity. Groups of students might also be assigned to present alternative analyses of a case based on different perspectives (e.g., parent versus student or teacher).

If you have never used cases in courses, some cautionary notes are in order. For most cases, there are no simple right or wrong answers to the discussion questions presented. Also, there is no easy way to predict what will happen to the youth or what type of approach will work best. One of the major goals in using case studies is to get students to use the theories, research, and concepts to think about possible interpretations and outcomes related to the case and learn to support their interpretations with evidence from the case or from their research.

If you have used cases in previous courses but are accustomed to short cases that emphasize a problem-based approach, you may at first be mystified by the cases in this book. While many of our cases present youth who are facing or have faced challenges in their lives, few of the cases present these challenges as the sole focus of the case. There usually is no single problem to solve in the cases; sometimes the case provides insight into how many problems have already been resolved. We encourage our students to think about the multiple issues, relationships, and events that have contributed to the past development of each child and adolescent and about what they need for healthy development in the future. This reflects our belief that developmental theories and research should help students analyze what helps or hinders the overall development of children and how one might build on the strengths and resources that these children possess.

Benefits of Using Case Studies

There has been extensive research on the benefits of using case studies in teaching. Most of the research on the case method has focused on the use of cases in general educational psychology courses, field experiences, or courses on learning, teaching methods, classroom management, or special education (Allen, 1995; Block, 1996; Mostert & Kauffman, 1992; Semrau & Fitzgerald, 1995; Sudzina, 1997; Sykes & Bird, 1993–1994; Wasserman, 1994). Relatively few articles have discussed the use of cases in courses on child and adolescent development (Corcoran, 1996; Mayo, 2002; McManus, 1986). However, the results of this research indicate the rich potential of case studies in providing an authentic context for considering problems that arise in working with children (Gibson, 1998; Hutchings, 1993; Kleinfeld, 1991; Merseth, 1991, 1994; Shulman, 1992; Sykes & Bird, 1993–1994; Vitz, 1990; Wasserman, 1994). We summarize this research below and provide references to it at the end of this book for persons who wish to explore the research more fully.

The research suggests that students benefit in several important ways from the use of cases in teaching. Case methods encourage development of student skills in communication, problem solving, decision making, collaboration, and conflict resolution (Hutchings, 1993; Kleinfeld, 1991; Merseth, 1991, 1994; Shulman, 1992; Sykes & Bird, 1993–1994; Wasserman, 1994). They also provide a way of broadening student experience with diverse settings and groups that may not be immediately available to them (LaFramboise & Griffith, 1997; Merseth, 1991; Roth, 2000). Cases also provide an authentic context that students report makes learning of content and abstract information easier (Sudzina, 1997). Our colleague James Allen (1995) reports research that cases lead to more active involvement by students in learning and an increased ability to understand the perspectives of others. Levin (1995) analyzed student learning while using cases and reported that discussion of cases resulted in more multidimensional understanding of issues, reductions in judgmental attitudes, and increased ability to take both the teacher and student perspectives. All of these outcomes are clearly desirable in teaching about human development.

We have found that our students enjoy both reading and analyzing case studies. They feel that the cases are "real" and become quite passionate in arguing for their interpretation and recommended actions. We have had students approach us a year after the course with details of the case fresh in their minds, asking us if we know what became of Ben, Elena, or Hector. It takes practice by the students and guidance from the instructor for students to develop the higher-order skills needed in case analysis. However, they leave the course with a much fuller appreciation of the value of theories and research as tools for understanding children and planning approaches to assist their development. We do suggest caution against generalizing too broadly about the lessons learned from individual life histories and cases. Not every autistic child will look like Emily and not every African American child will show the same characteristics as Keisha or Edward. However, we hope that by getting to know these children, you will develop skills that help you build a better future for all of the children that you meet.

CHART OF CASES

Ch.	Name/Title	Gender	Age	Race/Ethnicity	Family Background & Setting	Primary Issues	Secondary Issues	Possible Theorists/Theory for Discussion
1	Ben: Having His Way at Preschool and Home	M	4	Caucasian	Two-parent family One younger sibling Private, religious, pre-K school in urban setting	Social skill development Social cognition Peer and family relationships Kindergarten readiness	Cognitive and language development Self-perception Teacher-student interaction Play Family-school relations Classroom management	Piaget Vygotsky Erikson
2	Keisha: Connecting Across Differences	F	5	African American	Two-parent family Only child Private girls' school in urban setting	Emotional development Empathy Prosocial behavior Racial/ethnic awareness and identity	Cognitive development and language development Parenting styles Same-sex schooling Developmental issues for only children	Erikson Bronfenbrenner
3	Laura: Exploring Social and Creative Potentials in a Six-Year-Old's Life	F	6	Caucasian	Two-parent family Two siblings, middle child Public school in suburban setting	Social cognition Need for approval Play and cognitive development Middle child	Parenting Parental involvement in school Development of social skills (empathy) Friendships Sibling relationships	Piaget Vygotsky Gardner Bandura
4	Emily's World: Nurturing a Child With Autism	F	6	Caucasian	Two-parent family Two siblings, oldest child Public school in urban setting	The nature and wide range of manifestations of autistic disorder Theory of mind/metacognition Parenting a child with autism Treatments of autistic disorder	Theories regarding the causes of autism Operant behavior therapy Reinforcement as a motivator Developmental effects of having a sibling with disabilities	Bronfenbrenner Skinner

(Continued)

CHART OF CASES (Continued)

Ch.	Name/Title	Gender	Age	Race/Ethnicity	Family Background & Setting	Primary Issues	Secondary Issues	Possible Theorists/Theory for Discussion
5	Nicole and Brooke: Homeschooled Fraternal Twins	F	9	Caucasian and Puerto Rican	Two-parent family Fraternal twins, no other siblings Homeschooling in suburban setting	Sociocultural influences on cognitive development Twins and sibling relationships Homeschooling Nature versus nurture	Attachment Early physical development Personality and temperament Learning styles Friendship	Vygotsky
6	Beth: Finding Her Strengths	F	11	Caucasian	Two-parent family Second youngest of four girls Public school in urban setting	Cognitive development Academic difficulties Self-concept/ self-esteem Industry vs. inferiority	Moral development Teacher/parental expectations The effects of birth order on development, sibling relationships Presence of a stable, caring adult figure Friendship, peer acceptance	Piaget Information Processing Erikson Kohlberg
7	Edward: Full of Life and Always Moving	M	12	African American	Stepfamily living with grandmother One younger sister Academic-focused summer camp in urban setting	Attention deficit hyperactivity disorder and the influence of context on youth with disabilities Social and emotional development Out-of-school activities Mentoring, adult/youth relationships, mediated learning	Social cognition and social skills Multicultural friendships Peer relationships	Erikson Vygotsky Gardner

CHART OF CASES (Continued)

Ch.	Name/Title	Gender	Age	Race/Ethnicity	Family Background & Setting	Primary Issues	Secondary Issues	Possible Theorists/Theory for Discussion
8	Frank: Confronting Change and Taking a Stand in Middle School	M	13	Caucasian	Two-parent family Two older sisters (oldest is grown stepsister, not living at home) Public school in rural setting	Depression Identity development Peer groups/peer pressure/cliques/social isolation Moral development	Empathy, prosocial behaviors Motivation strategies	Bronfenbrenner Kohlberg Maslow
9	Talisha: Overcoming Loss With a New Family	F	13	African American	Death of mother due to crack cocaine addiction Single-parent family, nonfamilial guardian Public elementary school in urban setting	Mother's cocaine addiction and later death Guardianship assumed by neighbor Single-parent family Support networks of family and neighbors Academic motivation	Sibling relationships Attachment Religion Educational reform and low-income schools Middle school education	Erikson Bandura Bronfenbrenner
10	Elena: Surviving Family Problems	F	16	Puerto Rican	Single-parent family (mother) Public high school in urban setting	Adolescent identity development—especially with respect to peers, career choice, family relationships, dating, ethnicity, and conflicts with authorities Friendship, peer relationships, and ethnic conflicts The effects of alcoholism on the family	Physical self-concept and body image Domestic violence Motivation and school achievement Teacher and student relationships Problems faced by gay, lesbian, and bisexual students and how schools address these problems	Erikson

(Continued)

CHART OF CASES (Continued)

Ch.	Name/Title	Gender	Age	Race/Ethnicity	Family Background & Setting	Primary Issues	Secondary Issues	Possible Theorists/Theory for Discussion
11	Hector: Talking Through Troubles	M	17	Mexican American (immigrant)	Two-parent family One sibling, younger brother Public high school in urban setting	Resiliency Teacher-student relationships Social isolation/social development Effects of domestic and community violence on development	Cultural values Loss of loved ones/friends to violence Depression	Bandura
12	Jaime: Crossing Cultures and Celebrating Life	M	18	Mexican American (immigrant)	Single-parent and stepfamily Two siblings—younger sister and younger stepbrother Teenage father Public high school in urban setting	Identity development Resiliency Social skills Social support networks Bicultural competence	Immigrant children and families Motivation Teenage parenthood Parenting styles	Bronfenbrenner Erikson Vygotsky

CONNECTING ACROSS CASES

The following questions address issues that can be examined across cases. In some instances, specific cases are suggested. Other questions are open-ended and allow you to select cases for analysis. We suggest that you use the chart preceding these questions to determine which cases would best fit the open-ended questions.

1. Keisha and Laura are two young girls with very strong social skills, while Ben seems to struggle with his social development. Compare these cases in terms of how gender, parenting, teacher's classroom management and instructional styles, school context, social values, or other factors might have influenced the children's development.

2. Teachers play significant roles in the lives of all children. Select two cases in which you think teachers used approaches that promoted a child's cognitive, social, emotional, or moral growth. Discuss why their approaches were successful with that child.

3. The larger social context often plays a critical role in development. Select two youth growing up in two different types of neighborhoods or schools. Discuss how their neighborhood or school influenced their social, emotional, moral, or cognitive development.

4. Several of the youth commented directly or indirectly on the events of the September 11 terrorist attacks or the subsequent wars in Afghanistan and Iraq (i.e., Keisha, Laura, Brooke and Nicole, Beth, Frank). Select two of the youth and characterize their reactions to these events. In what ways were the reactions of the youth typical of their developmental levels? What does research suggest about ways that teachers and families should approach this issue and the issue of loss of a loved one?

5. The youth in these cases vary in their motivation and academic achievement. Select two youth who show different levels of motivation or academic achievement. Discuss the factors that might account for these differences, including consideration of age-related differences, family influences, school context, teacher-student relationships, and teacher's instructional approaches.

6. Family structures in the United States are quite varied and include single- and two-parent families, stepfamilies, and extended families. Developmentalists insist that any structure can provide a healthy environment for child development as long as the family has sufficient support and resources. Select two to three cases that have different family structures at some time in the child's life. Discuss how the families did or did not create a supportive, loving, and stimulating environment for these children.

7. Hector and Jaime are both youth whose families emigrated to the United States from Mexico to provide a better future for their children. In what ways do these youth show the influence of both U.S. and Mexican cultural values in their lives? What types of challenges did the parents and youth face due to immigration and the parents' limited English abilities? How did the teachers of each youth show or not show cultural sensitivity to their cultural backgrounds?

8. Resiliency is the ability to thrive despite adverse situations. Elena, Hector, Talisha, and Jaime might all be considered youth who have shown an ability to rise to meet the challenges in their lives. Discuss how the cases for these youth include personal, family, or community characteristics associated with resilience.

9. Animals play a prominent role in the lives of Ben, Brooke and Nicole, Beth, and Frank. Search for research on how pets and farm animals might influence children's development, then examine how you might apply this research to the cases noted.

ONE

BEN

Having His Way at Preschool and Home

———◄•◆•►———

PRIMARY AND SECONDARY ISSUES

Primary Issues:	*Secondary Issues:*
• Social skill development	• Cognitive and language development
• Social cognition	• Self-perception
• Peer and family relationships	• Teacher-student interaction
• Kindergarten readiness	• Play
	• Family-school relations
	• Classroom management

CASE

"Playing on the computer is my favorite thing to do," says Ben in a firm and very convincing voice. Ben, who is nearly four, confidently goes on to explain that his favorite computer game is *Horton the Elephant.* This is a game he plays at Uncle Mike's, who often baby-sits for Ben when his mom is at school. His face is beaming as he describes his visits to Uncle Mike. "My Uncle Mike lets me play on his computer whenever I want," shouts a very excited Ben.

Besides playing on the computer, Ben likes to play outside. In particular, he enjoys riding his "super wheels" that his grandfather gave him. He and his father had to put it together. "It was all in pieces," exclaims Ben. "My daddy and I made the handle and then we made the pedal and everything we need on it." Ben is proud of his accomplishment and of the work he did with his dad. Remembering the first time he rode his bike, he reminds his mother that she forgot to put his helmet on. He says with authority that you have to wear a helmet so "when ya hurt your head, your head won't get hurt. It's just for safety keeping."

Ben is the older of two children. His younger brother, Tyler, is about 18 months old, and they sometimes get into tangles with each other. Mom reports that Ben "doesn't like Tyler to touch anything he doesn't want him to," which seems like just about everything. He makes his little brother aware of his desires by "screaming" at him. He likes to be in charge and to tell his little brother exactly what to do. If Tyler doesn't comply, sometimes the screaming can escalate into physical contact. When Tyler persists, Ben may just knock him over to prevent him from getting his toys. However, even in the same play setting you might see a nurturing side of Ben directed toward Tyler. He loves to hug his brother and can be very protective of him. He says that sometimes he just has to "block" Tyler from getting things that might hurt him. For example, one day Ben noticed that Tyler was about to get into some shoe polish that was on the couch. Ben says, "I needed to protect him because if he got it, he would put it in his mouth and brush it in his mouth and he would cough." So Ben just "blocked" Tyler's access to the couch. In fact, the blocking is something he really likes to do. "I kind of like blocking the way, but when Tyler gets bigger than me, he'll do it with his head." Ben doesn't seem to be overly concerned about his brother getting too much bigger than he. He laughs and says, "Every time Tyler grows, I grow bigger."

Ben will very affectionately tell you that there is a special bed in his room for Tyler when he gets bigger. He is looking forward to the time when Tyler is big enough to sleep on the bottom bunk. Interestingly, when talking about his relationship to Tyler, Ben becomes a bit confused. When he is asked if he (Ben) has a brother, he is quick to respond yes. Then when asked if Tyler has a brother, he initially pauses and says "um, no." Then he continues, "Not, um, I am his brother but he doesn't have another brother yet." When his mother asks, "What about you?" he finally says, "Yes, Tyler has a brother and it is me."

Ben is anxiously waiting for his fourth birthday, which is coming up in a few weeks. He talks about the upcoming party and the presents he might receive. He is looking forward to a party with mostly family and a few friends. He thinks very carefully about what he would like for his birthday. "Last year,

I wanted a magic school bus, but my mom didn't let me." However, Mom has no recollection of such a request. When she tells this to Ben, he laughs, "I was just tricking you." But on his last birthday there was a very special birthday present from Ben's uncle. It was down in his uncle's basement. "We cannot go down there now, so I will just gotta tell you." Ben describes it as "a real, it's a horsey but it's really not real or alive, um, you just pick it up and pretend—it's make believe." When asked if he rides the horse, Ben replies confidently, "Yes." But he seems a bit confused about the horse. He goes on to describe the present as really being two horses. He turns to his mom and asks, "They are not real, right Mommy?" Mom replies that Ben is right and, when asked what make believe horses are, he states, "That means you're riding something, you're making, you're pretending they are real and alive. But it is not this way, that's make believe."

Talking with Ben about his family, one gets a sense that he is a man in control of his destiny and very aware of everything going on in his home. His house is in a residential section of an urban community. He lives there with his mom, dad, brother, and his dog. He reports that he has a new house, but it got very old. "It's old because our house is fixed . . . and in a storm a branch fell and hit the wire and then fell on our house and it got very old." He delighted in watching the repairmen fix the wire leading to the house.

As far as his dog is concerned, Ben loves to help care for her. He says that "big brothers take care of dogs," and he is often called upon to let the dog outside to go "potty." He reports that pets have to go to the bathroom outside. In fact, he asserts that his aunt's dog "never needs to go potty when he is inside."

When Ben is not playing outside, playing on the computer, or playing with his brother, he often asks others to read to him. He explains, "I can't read all of my books." He reports that his favorite book is *There is an Alligator Under My Bed.* He particularly likes the little boy in the book. This little boy is his favorite character because "he puts food and drinks on the ground for the alligator." He talks about the alligator as though it was the little boy's pet and explains that sometimes the alligator stays under the boy's bed or in the garage. Ben seems to like the fact that the little boy is taking good care of his pet alligator, much like he takes care of his dog.

Superheroes are so "cool," according to Ben. His favorite superhero is Superman, but he also likes Superman's friends Spiderman, Batman, and Aquaman. He thinks it is great that Superman has so many friends. He enjoys watching these superheroes on television but also reports enjoying *Oswald the*

Octopus. It seems that Oswald has a good friend, Pongo, that Ben also likes. Pongo is a gentle dragon, and Ben really likes the fact that Pongo is so friendly.

When is comes to his own friends, Ben seems to struggle a bit. He talks about some female playmates in the neighborhood who are friendly toward him. However, when he talks about school friends, he describes them with mixed emotions. Sometimes the kids are friendly, but sometimes the "kids are not so friendly and nice."

Ben goes to a religious preschool operated by a local synagogue and has been in a mixed-gender class of three- and four-year-olds for two years now. Ben's preschool serves 40 families who are mostly Caucasian and of middle or high socioeconomic status. The school focuses on both Judaic and secular studies. He says that he usually likes school, especially when they go to the park, sing, and make things. However, Ben adamantly reports that he does not like it when his teachers (he has three) put him in time out. He explains that time out is something that happens when he misbehaves. He knows that the one misbehavior that results in being placed in time out is growling at his classmates or teachers. He only growls when he is "mad" and his teachers are "mean." Ben proudly states that he never really fights with his friends at school. After thinking about that for a while, he then says that he sometimes fights with them "when they don't be nice to me." When these classmates are not nice to him, they "pretend to be dragons and bad guys." One time, a few of his classmates "hit him with a stick at school." Ben says that when this happened he went to his teacher and told her that the kids had hit him. Apparently the teacher was talking to another teacher and did not listen to him. But Ben points out that even when "I said 'excuse me,' she still didn't listen." Ben repeats his feeling that he was not treated fairly and that when he says "excuse me" to someone he expects that person to listen to him.

However, when Ben comes into school, he strolls in confidently and walks right over to the cubby area to put his coat away. He greets his teachers with a big smile and a "hi" and walks over to the refrigerator to put his lunch away. A few classmates say "hi" and Ben responds, but does not seem overly anxious to get involved in a conversation or in a play activity with them. His mom sits down with him as he plays with a complicated puzzle. As he plays with the puzzle, he talks out loud to himself. It almost sounds like babbling. When another child approaches to play with the puzzle, Ben makes it very clear that his intention is to play with the puzzle alone. He remains on task for about four to five minutes, and during that time Mom kisses him good-bye and leaves. He smiles at her, and she reminds him that his favorite uncle will be picking him up after school. Ben smiles once again and waves good-bye to her. Ben continues working intently on the puzzle as other classmates arrive. His teacher comments that Ben has an incredible attention span and he can remain focused for long periods of time when he is enjoying an activity.

Ben's isolated play continues as two female classmates approach him. He reminds them that they may play with the puzzle when he is done. When one of the girls drops a toy on the floor, Ben offers to help. The other little girl says, "No, we do not need your help." One of the teachers overhears this conversation and reminds the girls how nice it was that Ben offered to help. Within a few minutes, the three children are working on the puzzle together. Ben takes the lead, offering suggestions on where to put the puzzle pieces. Suddenly, Ben decides it might be fun to put the puzzle pieces on the floor. The girls decide this is a grand idea and join in the fun. After a few minutes, however, Ben expresses annoyance at the girls. He no longer wants them to put the puzzle pieces on the floor and tells them so. They ignore him and he starts growling at them, a behavior for which Ben is often scolded by his teachers. One of the teachers comes over and asks the children to pick up the puzzle pieces. Ben ignores the teacher's request as the girls quickly comply. The teacher then repeats the request to Ben and after some coaxing, he also complies.

Ben then joins his classmates who are working together to build a tower in the gross motor play area. Initially, when Ben enters, his classmates seem somewhat reluctant to let him join in, telling each other he "will just knock down whatever we build." However, they let him help, and Ben chatters to himself the entire time. He sings a song and says some rhymes as he plays with the children and does not really have any conversation with his classmates. He appears to be delighted to be included in the play activity. Apparently, however, Ben becomes bored and begins to knock some of the blocks over. The other children initially join in (it seems like a good idea to most of them), but then they express their annoyance when Ben refuses to stop. The children move on to another activity, and Ben continues knocking down the blocks, this time all alone.

Ben seems to know when he is not welcome in an activity. He is quick to point out who likes him and who does not like him. When he senses he is not welcome, he resorts to growling at his classmates and tries to interrupt their play. This makes his classmates more annoyed with him, and they try to ignore him or they simply tell their teacher that he is being "bad."

Ms. Silver, the head teacher in Ben's classroom, holds an advanced degree, as do all the head teachers at Ben's preschool. As a group, these teachers have an average of 10 years of teaching experience. The preschool classroom is divided into two rooms, one essentially devoted to gross motor development and the other to the development of fine motor skills. A myriad of toys and activities are always prepared for the children before they enter in the morning. There is a focus on cooperation and the development of self-control using a system of rewards and punishments. The children receive positive feedback whenever they are engaged in appropriate behavior. Negative feedback and time out are often used to control and minimize undesirable behavior. When asked to describe Ben, Ms. Silver says that he is an "adorable child" who is very bright (IQ score of 130 as measured by WIPPSI) and keenly aware of his surroundings. She indicates that he is very polite when he comes into school in the morning, greeting and saying hello to everyone. "He has very strong verbal skills; however, he is socially quite young," says Ms. Silver. One of the behaviors she is particularly concerned with is his tendency to "get into the faces" of other kids. He knows "exactly whose face to get into." She says that while she has tried various techniques to eliminate the behavior, nothing has seemed to work. She praises him when he is playing cooperatively with the other children. She has also tried a time out when he is behaving inappropriately and tells him that his behavior hurts others' feelings. She explicitly tries to tie the "in your face behavior" to the hurt feelings of others. Ms. Silver says that Ben does not seem to care and that the reprimand does not appear to make any difference to him. She describes him as "physical" at times and "somewhat mischievous." When he plays, he constantly talks to himself. Ms. Silver describes this as "nervous chatter." She says that sometimes he talks so much that she has to remind him that he needs to give *her* a chance to talk.

Another concern of Ms. Silver is when Ben disrupts the play of others or disrupts a group activity. Her observations lead her to conclude that he lacks the social skills necessary to gain entrance into a play activity. While he is extremely verbal, he does not use those skills when he is trying to play with others. If he tries to join a group play activity and is rebuffed, he simply growls and then disrupts the children's play. Ms. Silver says that his classmates then "turn off to him and do not want to play with him." He often then goes off and plays by himself and leaves the group play to others.

Ben's parents are quite involved in the education of their son, particularly Mom who takes Ben to school. They are concerned parents and have had some conversations with Ms. Silver, although it is only the second month of the school year. His parents report that they are happy with the religious school, especially its director and the structure of his classroom. Mom feels very strongly that Ben needs a structured classroom. He needs to have a time to do one thing, and a time to move on to something else. She says that the home-school communication is good this year, "much better than last year" when he had a different teacher at the same school. A conference is planned in a few weeks and one of the topics of conversation will be Ben's social skill development and his readiness for kindergarten. In a passing conversation with Ben's mom, Ms. Silver found out that Mom was looking at different kindergarten programs. While Ms. Silver believes that Ben has made tremendous progress over the first several months of this year, she is concerned that socially he might not be ready for kindergarten. She believes that Ben is clearly ready to do the academic work of kindergarten, but his social skills need to be further developed. She is likely going to recommend another year of nursery school, especially given the fact that he is just turning four. This is a point she believes she and Ben's mom will disagree on.

Ms. Silver says that she has tried different things to get Ben to cooperate. For example, during the first weeks of school the bell would ring for the children to come in when they were out on the playground. When the bell would ring, Ben would run and get under the playground equipment. At first, she tried running after him and quickly realized that this was not working. She would run and he would run faster. She then tried a different approach. She told Ben that the entire class was going in and he would be the only one left on the playground. As she took the class in (keeping her eye on Ben the entire time), Ben realized that no one was going to run after him. "He watched us leave and then suddenly decided to join us. The next time we went out on the playground, I just reminded him what happened the last time the bell rang and he came right in." Apparently it has not been a problem since then.

Mom describes Ben in some ways that are similar to Ms. Silver's report. She says that he is "very intelligent" and indicates that his personality is "charismatic" and that "he loves people." Mom is in her mid 20s and is currently a college student looking to graduate at the end of next semester. Dad is in his late 20s and works for a government agency. Dad is very interested in sports and also likes to sing. Mom is pretty busy raising two children and attending school. They do many things together as a family, such as TV watching, playing outside, playing in the basement, going to the park, and going to the movies. Mom describes Ben's brother as being more strong-willed and headstrong than Ben. She describes their relationship as close and says that Ben really "loves Tyler." In fact, one of her fondest memories of Ben is the first time he met Tyler. Ben was about two and a half when Tyler was born. His first comment was, "Oh, there is my baby brother. Oh, look at his little hands and his little feet and his little toes. Can I hold him?" At that moment there was no jealousy, and Ben acted as if he had waited too long for this special arrival.

That doesn't mean there is no sibling rivalry. Mom indicates that there is "definite rivalry, but it depends on the moment." For example, she points out that Ben "doesn't like Tyler to touch anything or do anything he doesn't want him to do." Ben likes to be the "one in charge and tell Tyler exactly what to do." When Tyler does not comply (which happens often), Ben will scream at him or "play fight." Ben will "tackle Tyler," but for the most part they are "pretty good with each other."

Like Ms. Silver, Mom describes Ben as extremely verbal. She says that he talks constantly and that their conversations range from talking about death to talking about how much they love each other. Mom believes that Ben has a good understanding of death. Ben's grandfather, with whom he had a very special relationship, died when Ben was only 15 months old. Mom has taken Ben to the cemetery and explained that his grandfather is dead. Ben has told her that when someone dies, they go up to God, are with God, and are not coming back to earth. While he does not dwell on the topic of death, Ben seems to be aware of its finality.

When talking about Ben's social skills, Mom has some real concerns. She says that his "social skills are a little lacking with his peers." Like Ms. Silver, Mom believes that Ben has difficulty initiating play activities with other children. He appears to "be rigid and I just wish he would be more flexible," says Mom. He does not appear to want to compromise with his peers and wants his own way. Mom says that Ben does have one good friend at school with whom he shares very similar interests. They apparently play pretty well together until the little friend does something that Ben doesn't want him to do. For the most part, she believes that he is "kind of a loner, unless kids want to do what he wants to do."

As far as family disagreements, Mom says that there are a few things "that really push Ben's buttons." "Don't give him the wrong food, and don't refuse his request to watch television before bed." If he is not permitted to watch television before bed, he will just refuse to go upstairs to bed and will tell his mom that she is making him "very angry." The technique that Mom uses is to count and tell Ben that if he is not upstairs when she is finished counting, he will not get a bedtime story. He then gets into an argument with her and begs her not to count. "He thinks that if I don't count, then he has as much time as he wants." When she finally gets him upstairs, the next struggle is to pick a book. She tries to give him a choice of a few different books, but usually he doesn't want one of the books she has picked. He looks around his room trying to pick out a book. When Mom tries to get him to make a choice he becomes angry. She tells him that if he has not picked out a book by the time she counts to 10, she is not reading to him. This may cause an angry outburst, and bedtime becomes a difficult experience. It comes down to not getting his way. He will just "scream and cry," but if she keeps repeating, "Ben, it's bedtime," eventually he will "wind down" and go to sleep.

She hopes that in the future Ben will learn to compromise. She worries that he will be the kid who won't sit in his chair and is always in the principal's office because he wants to do what he wants to do. She hopes he will learn to meet people "half way," and have an easy life in which he does well and accomplishes what he wants to do. Hopefully, Ben will.

DISCUSSION QUESTIONS

1. What aspects of language has Ben mastered? What language skills is he still developing? Give specific examples from the case.

2. How would you characterize Ben's play activities? In what ways has his play influenced his social, cognitive, and language development?

3. Socially, Ben appears to struggle with friendships and peer relationships. What do you believe has influenced his difficulties? Be sure to consider his relationships with adults, contextual factors, and cognitive development in your explanation.

4. In what ways have Ben's mom and his teacher tried to enhance his social skill development? If you were Ben's mom or teacher, what else would you do to deal with his inappropriate social behavior? Justify your actions from a theoretical or research perspective.

5. Evaluate the mother's and teacher's positions on Ben's readiness for kindergarten. What would you do if you were making this decision?

What additional information would you want to have? Support your answer from a research and theoretical perspective.

6. How would you characterize Ben's self-perception? What do you believe influenced Ben's view of himself?

7. What appear to be positive and negative reinforcers for Ben? Do his mother and teacher use reinforcement effectively? Why or why not? What other approaches to discipline do they use?

APPLYING THEORETICAL PERSPECTIVES

1. Using Social Cultural (Vygotsky), Cognitive Development (Piaget), and Information Processing theories, analyze Ben's cognitive development. In particular, how would Vygotsky and Piaget differ in their perspectives on the role of peers in Ben's development and in their perspectives on Ben's talking to himself?

2. Summarize Ben's progress through the earlier stages of personal and emotional and cognitive development described by Erikson. Thus far, has he overcome the various "crises" described by Erikson? Cite specific evidence from the case to support your answers.

3. According to Piaget's theory of cognitive development, at what stage is Ben likely functioning? Support your answer with specific examples from the case.

Also see "Connecting Across Cases" question 9, in the Introduction to this book.

CLASS ACTIVITIES

1. Role-play the discussion between Ben's mother and his teacher regarding Ben's readiness for kindergarten. Include both cognitive and social development issues in your discussion. Also consider how his mother and teacher might work together to increase his readiness.

2. Role-play bedtime at Ben's house, paying particular attention to Mom's handling of the situation. Demonstrate both effective and ineffective methods of discipline.

3. Role-play a discussion between Ben's parents and teachers in which they develop a joint plan for addressing his social development problems.

RESEARCH SUGGESTION

1. Do children who are gifted experience more problems in peer relationships than children who are not? Explain your answer, citing current research on gifted children. How might it apply to this case?

READINGS AND RESOURCES

The Parent Center Web site at www.parentcenter.com/kindergarten-readiness

This Web site provides information for parents to assist in the assessment of a child's readiness to enter kindergarten. It provides essential information about the necessary skills for success in kindergarten and how to prepare children for their kindergarten experience.

Preschoolers Today Web site at www.preschoolerstoday.com/resources/readykinder.htm

A simple assessment tool that can be used by parents to evaluate kindergarten readiness.

Sankar-DeLeeuw, N. (2002). Gifted preschoolers: Parent and teacher views on identification, early admission, and programming. *Roeper Review 24*(3), 172–177.

An examination of the issues and concerns of parents and teachers of gifted preschoolers, with a focus on early identification and programming.

Webb, J. T. (1994). Nurturing social emotional development of gifted children. Reston, VA: ERIC Clearinghouse on Disabilities and Gifted Education. (ERIC Document Reproduction Service No. ED372554) Retrieved June 12, 2004, from www.ericfacility.net/ericdigests/ed372554.html

An analysis of the problems and issues facing gifted children.

TWO

KEISHA

Connecting Across Differences

———◆———

PRIMARY AND SECONDARY ISSUES

Primary Issues:	*Secondary Issues:*
• Emotional development	• Cognitive development and language development
• Empathy	• Parenting styles
• Prosocial behavior	• Same-sex schooling
• Racial/ethnic awareness and identity	• Developmental issues for only children

CASE

It is 7:45 A.M. and Keisha beams as she walks into her kindergarten classroom. The classroom, adorned with holiday decorations representing many cultures, is warm and welcoming. It is situated at the end of a long hallway in a wing devoted to early childhood education. Keisha's obvious enthusiasm for school appears to be shared by the other 12 girls in her classroom. Dressed in plaid jumpers and navy blue shoes (part of the school uniform), the girls giggle as they put away their coats and exchange morning greetings. Ms. Sommers, the head teacher, begins to sing a welcome song and the 13 girls make their way to the brightly colored rug situated in front of the piano. The song serves as a cue that Ms. Sommers is ready to begin the morning activities. Keisha, the first student to the rug, begins the circle with her classmates following close behind. She sits as close to Ms. Sommers and the piano as she can get. Ms. Sommers welcomes everyone to a new school day and checks with the class to see if anyone has interesting news to share. Hands wave excitedly and many girls, including Keisha, have a story to tell. Ms. Sommers carefully listens to each of them and makes certain that they are all being good listeners as each girl shares her "news." Keisha is excited to tell her classmates that the guest in the class that morning—me—is a friend of hers. She comes over and sits on my lap while the other girls watch carefully. Ms. Sommers then redirects the girls to the circle activities and begins a conversation about the first project of the day. Since the winter holiday season is approaching, the girls' first activity is a winter art project using glue, glitter, and brightly colored paper and feathers. When Ms. Sommers is finished with her instructions, Keisha jumps up, puts on her smock, and appears ready to begin. Ms. Sommers thanks the class for being good listeners and sends them to the art materials, which are neatly laid out on a large art table. All the students, including Keisha, proceed with their art activity with great focus and interest. Ms. Sommers and her assistant, Ms. Turner, walk around the room, checking on the progress of the students. One kindergarten student, who is socializing and not working on her art project, is quickly redirected in a positive and caring manner.

Keisha is a bright eyed and bubbly five-year-old, and the only African American enrolled in an all-day kindergarten program at this private school for girls. She is the youngest student in this small and nurturing community of 13 learners. The K–12 enrollment of this selective admission school is approximately 350 students, and the school is a fully accredited independent school approved by the state board of education. Keisha, an only child of two professional parents, lives in a middle-class urban neighborhood in the northeast United States. She has her own bedroom and happily reports that "[I] make my bed a lot" and "[I] like to jump on the bed." She often brings her dolls to bed with her although "they all get in my pillow." In addition to Mom and Dad, Keisha has two pet birds, Raven and Wings, who fly around the house. "I can't play with them," and "they always fly on the couch," she reports, and proudly adds, "I help Mom and Dad take care of them." Keisha's parents come from close-knit families who all enjoy spending time with her. According to her dad, "she loves to spend time with her cousins, aunts, uncles, and grandparents." Keisha describes her mom as a special lady because "when I cry she picks me up and I feel better." Keisha enjoys playing basketball with her dad and especially enjoys their reading time together, even though "he sometimes yells." Dad says the times he yells at Keisha are "few and far between." He does recall one time when he did raise his voice to her. She "stuck her fingers in an air purifier" and needed to be rushed to the hospital for treatment. Keisha's dad says they prefer to discipline her by "setting boundaries, negotiating, and working things out. I don't believe in spanking or a lot of yelling."

One of Keisha's favorite activities to do with her mom and dad is to read books. *Little Mermaid* is a story she never gets tired of hearing. Ariel, the mermaid, is her favorite character. "Ariel is my favorite because she wants to know everything and 'cause she gets the prince." *Aladdin* is another Disney book Keisha enjoys hearing. Aladdin, her favorite character, "lives in a marketplace and doesn't have real clothes. He just wears a jacket and ragged pants." When she is asked why Aladdin is so special, Keisha affectionately says, "Because he saves the day."

Saving the day is something Keisha has obviously thought about. At five years old she has decided that "when I grow up I want to be a police officer." She wants to be a police officer because it is "something we really, really, really need. They keep people safe and so do firefighters." (Note this interview was done just a few months after the terrorist attacks on September 11, 2001.) When asked what she knew about the events of September 11, Keisha's knowledge was limited to people getting hurt and police and firefighters being heroes. Her parents minimized her exposure to the realities of September 11 by limiting her television viewing.

The student population of Keisha's school is predominantly white and affluent. While the school administration is committed to increasing the school's diversity (several outreach programs have been instituted), the number of African American girls remains low. However, the school does have some socioeconomic diversity. Many of the girls who attend the costly school receive financial assistance. The lack of racial diversity at the school was an early concern of Keisha's parents. Dad says that he was "a bit concerned about the need for diversity in where [Keisha] went to school." He is less worried now that he knows more about the school and its environment. He sees the diversity in "backgrounds and ideologies" as an important aspect of Keisha's education, although he indicates that Keisha is beginning to talk about the ethnic and racial makeup of her school. However, at this point both Mom and Dad believe that Keisha's school is a "good place for her to be and grow." The fact that she is always included in school activities, after-school activities, and "play dates" confirms this belief for Mom and Dad. Ms. Sommers agrees. She says that "while Keisha does notice racial differences, it is not an issue in this class." Ms. Sommers describes a particular incident that reflects Keisha's growing awareness of race. "Last week the girls were making angels as a holiday project and I had white faces, tan faces, and pink faces. She immediately went to the tan face and said 'this one is for me.' We do a lot with difference and acceptance." Keisha's own awareness is clear when she is asked how to make her school a better place. She smiles and says, "Getting more people here really, really like the whole world."

Ms. Sommers believes strongly that Keisha's school experiences have had a positive influence on her development. In fact, Ms. Sommers reports that Keisha "has blossomed" this year. This is the second year that Keisha and Ms. Sommers have been together. Ms. Sommers was the preschool teacher last year, and she and the school administration decided that she would move up to kindergarten along with the preschool girls. They believe that this policy encourages continuity of instruction and expectations, while allowing the teacher the opportunity to get to know the girls' strengths and weaknesses at this important developmental level. "Looping," as it is referred to in education literature, is strongly endorsed by the parents, administration, and the teachers. The girls seem to have no complaints either. Keisha loves her teacher because she "fixes problems."

Ms. Sommers believes that over the last year and a half, "Keisha has made a lot of growth with sounds and letters. Mom and Dad work with her at home and they are very invested in Keisha and this school." Dad says that "they make a point of asking her how her day was." Keisha will tell them "about the things that might have bothered her at school. It doesn't take a lot to get her to open up." She also loves to "present things that she has done during the day and projects she has done."

As is the case with most of the girls in this kindergarten class, Keisha clearly enjoys the hands-on activities and interactions with other students that Ms. Sommers provides throughout the day in her classroom. Ms. Sommers has provided various opportunities for Keisha and her classmates to engage in activities that both focus on and cross many subject areas and that are suited to each student's individual strengths and interests. Keisha does not seem to mind the academic work that is expected of the girls in this kindergarten classroom. She enthusiastically exclaims, "I like hard work. I love numbers and letters."

Keisha excels in the arts, music, and drama, and Ms. Sommers is certain that Keisha will be up on stage "in a future drama production." Her enjoyment of the arts is strongly encouraged and nurtured at home. Keisha is involved in an after-school dance program and loves to sing in her church choir. Keisha can look forward to many opportunities to participate in the arts at her school, where both visual and performing arts are highly valued activities.

Along with the academic part of school, Keisha loves to socialize. Ms. Sommers indicates that Keisha relates well to the other kids in the class and is extremely well liked. In fact, "she is the kind of kid you just fall in love with. She has a heart of gold and just gets along with everyone." However, Ms. Sommers says that her heart of gold can easily get broken. Ms. Sommers, who monitors classroom social behavior closely, says that if "someone is insensitive to her, she takes it to heart. If I have to discipline her [something that clearly does not happen often] she becomes very emotional."

This sensitive side of Keisha is evident to her parents. Her dad characterizes her as "a bright, capable, and physically competent child . . . who loves interacting with people." She is very open to the world around her and she's very trusting of people. She is concerned about the people around her being okay, and she understands what it means to have your feelings hurt.

Keisha echoes her father's characterization of her sensitivity. She has a close friend whose name is Patty. Patty, a friend from preschool who now attends a different school, is Keisha's good friend because "we sometimes do the same thing. We like to do flips and stuff and . . . she is funny." When describing some of her interactions with Patty, Keisha says that Patty is sometimes "mean" and that "sometimes Patty will say that 'I'm not going to be your friend' and stuff. A person's feelings can break when [you] are being mean to [them]." Keisha further describes what might happen if she has a fight with Patty or any of her other friends. According to Keisha, when people fight "some people come and say how about you just be nice or I [might] come over and say that. How about we be friends for the whole week?" Keisha also really likes her friends at school "because they are fun. Sometimes they can be mean too, like we can break, like they can break the people's feelings they are being mean to. When they might hurt somebody, well, somebody might say a bad thing." According to Keisha, this can be made better by "people getting back together . . . and love, lotta, lotta loving." These thoughts, and others like them, are what make Keisha happy. In fact, "people getting back together" is what makes her smile.

Sadness, anger, and fear are not emotions Keisha talks about very often. When she does talk about sadness, it is quite personalized. It makes "me sad when people don't listen to me and I'm trying to say something. That all breaks my heart." In fact, if people don't listen to her, her sadness sometimes turns into anger. "Sometimes, I get all red on my face. When people really, really, really don't listen to me." When asked when this anger surfaces, Keisha responds by saying "like on Mondays and Fridays."

Her fears come in the form of "vampires who suck your blood." She knows about vampires because "I just know." (Her parents really don't know what the source of this information is!) "Besides vampires, ghosts are really scary. They have no bones and no skin." Another "thing that makes me scared are witches." Keisha says she "can smile" when there are no vampires, ghosts, and witches.

Keisha's mom and dad and Ms. Sommers strongly believe that her greatest strengths involve her verbal ability, her desire to explore, her love of learning, and her willingness to try new and different things. In fact, her dad characterizes her as a bit of a risk taker. "She has been doing things outside on her jungle gym that make her mom a bit nervous. But I look at it as a manifestation of her physical competence."

These strong verbal and risk-taking skills became apparent at the end of her interview. Just before Keisha was ready to leave, she was asked if there was anything else she would like to share. Keisha looked up brightly and boldly took the microphone. She said now it was her turn to be the interviewer and take center stage. Speaking directly into the microphone, she asked me the following questions:

> What about your life? Is there anything you don't like? Do you have any kids? Where do they live? What makes you happy? What is your favorite drink? Have your children ever played any tricks on one another? Tell me one.

She not only understood the techniques of interviewing, she knew what questions to ask and decided if she was going to share her life, then I would have to share mine as well. Luckily, the tape ran out; the questions were being fired rapidly and getting more and more personal. Watch out, Katie Couric!

DISCUSSION QUESTIONS

1. Characterize the parenting style of Keisha's parents. Do Keisha's development and behavior seem consistent with what research says about the results of the parenting style you believe Keisha's parents exhibit? As parents of an African American child, what additional parenting issues might concern Keisha's parents?

2. Speculate on the changes that might occur in Keisha's development were she to have a younger sibling. Support your speculation with the results of research you have studied in class and in course materials.

3. Predict the effect on Keisha's future ethnic identity development should her school environment stay the same in terms of ethnic enrollment.

4. In what ways should the research on culturally relevant pedagogy influence the curriculum and instruction in Keisha's kindergarten classroom? What suggestions, based upon research, do you have for Keisha's teacher to help her create a truly inclusive environment?

APPLYING THEORETICAL PERSPECTIVES

1. Using clues from the case, outline Keisha's development through Erikson's stages of personal and emotional development. Thus far, has she overcome the various "crises" described by Erikson? What are they, and how would you characterize Keisha's resolution of these stages? In outlining Keisha's progress in these areas, detail what factors in Keisha's environment Bronfenbrenner would consider in analyzing Keisha's development.

2. What theoretical perspective(s) and theorist(s) within such perspective(s) (other than Erikson and Bronfenbrenner) provide the most insight into Keisha's cognitive, social, emotional, and physical development? Note that different perspectives and theorists may account for different areas of Keisha's development. Use details from the case and support your answer with information from the text. You may want to "map" or "chart" the various areas of Keisha's development in order to organize your thoughts.

3. What developmental theorist(s) is Ms. Sommers embracing in her classroom methods, and how is Keisha apparently responding to that environment? Be specific, using details from the case and details on the theorists from your course.

Also see "Connecting Across Cases" questions 1 and 4, in the Introduction to this book.

CLASS ACTIVITIES

1. Role-play Keisha's parents discussing the issues of ethnic diversity in the school with school administrator(s).

2. Role-play a discussion between Keisha's parents where one parent wants to remove her from her current school because ethnic enrollment has not changed whereas the other wants to keep her enrolled.

RESEARCH SUGGESTIONS

1. With a partner or small group, research the same-sex schooling movement and outline the pros and cons of same-sex schooling for the class.

2. Research the practice of "looping" in education, paying particular attention to results relating to its effects on cognitive, social, and emotional development, and present findings to the class.

3. Based on research on the development of empathy and prosocial behavior, role-play possible interactions between Keisha and her parents that support her caring behaviors and attitudes.

READINGS AND RESOURCES

National Coalition of Girls' Schools at www.ncgs.org

The NCGS is a coalition of girls' schools that advocates, supports, and provides resources on single-sex education for young women.

Haag, P. (2000). *K–12 single sex education: What does the research say?* Champaign, IL: ERIC Clearinghouse on Elementary and Early Childhood Education. (ERIC Document Reproduction Service No. ED 444758) Retrieved June 12, 2004, from www.ericfacility.net/ericdigests/ed444758.html

This ERIC Digest provides a summary of research on single-sex schools and children's academic progress and emotional development. It also identifies problems involved in doing research on single-sex schools.

Comer, J., & Poussaint, A. (1992). *Raising black children: Two leading psychiatrists confront the educational, social, and emotional problems facing black children.* New York: Penguin Books.

This book examines both general developmental issues in raising children and issues of particular relevance to African American children, including fostering racial and personal pride and coping with racism and discrimination.

Wright, M. (2000). *I'm chocolate, you're vanilla: Raising healthy black and biracial children in a race-conscious world.* San Francisco: Jossey-Bass.

This book discusses how young children develop an understanding of race and ethnicity and provides practical, positive suggestions for parents and teachers on handling common questions from children about race, responding to comments or actions by others to a child who is black or biracial, and reducing preconceptions about race that influence a child's success or failure.

LAURA

Exploring Social and Creative Potentials in a Six-Year-Old's Life

———•◦•◦•———

PRIMARY AND SECONDARY ISSUES

Primary Issues:	*Secondary Issues:*
• Social learning theory	• Parenting
• Social cognition	• Development of social
• Need for approval	skills (empathy)
• Play and cognitive	• Friendships
development	• Sibling relationships
	• Gardner's multiple intelligences

CASE

"My mom, dad, big sister, little sister, and puppy" is the way that six-year-old Laura describes the members of her family. Laura is the middle child in a family of three girls who live with their parents in a suburban community in the northeastern United States. Her parents are both professionals who work outside the home yet manage to devote a tremendous amount of time to family life. Laura's mom describes her marriage as a strong partnership in which both partners share the responsibilities and support of family life. "I can't remember the last time we [husband and wife] fought, so there is not much conflict in the house." Both parents stress the importance of education and the building of self-confidence in their girls. When purchasing their home, they selected the location partly because of the reputation of the school district. Laura's parents hope that their family and marriage will serve as models for the girls. They want their girls to recognize the importance of being full partners in a relationship built on respect, love, and commitment.

Laura describes herself as being "nice . . . and having lots of friends." She also says that she is a "sharing [person] and [is] good at skipping, running, . . . and gymnastics" and also feels "bad when other kids get into trouble at school." She is aware that she is the middle child in her family. However, the role of middle child does not seem to bother Laura at all. In fact, she says, "I am the middle one. I'm the big sister and the little one [sister], so I'm the one in the middle. I have a little sister to take care of and I [have] a big sister to take care of me." Laura's mom also describes her as the middle child, "but a much-awaited child. I had three miscarriages before her . . . she is kind of a treasure to us and she knows it." Laura's older sister Courtney and her younger sister Sarah are twelve and four. Laura shares a bedroom with Sarah and does not seem to mind it. However, she looks forward to the day she "turns seven when I get my own room." She is anxious to "decorate my own room like my big sister." All of this is news to her parents, who are currently not planning on a room change for the girls.

Laura feels close to her sisters, her parents, and her extended family and especially her grandfather, to whom she has a very special attachment. She says she is closest to "my mom and dad. My dad wrestles with me and my mom reads me bedtime stories." Her favorite books are by Dr. Seuss, and she especially loves *The Cat in the Hat*. Laura believes that her parents are special "because they love me." Laura speaks of her little sister Sarah with great affection. They enjoy playing games together which often involve pretend play. Her pretend play is enhanced by her strong imagination. In fact, according to her mom, Laura's imagination is "endless, just unbelievable . . . if you give [Laura] two rocks, she will play for hours."

One game, which Laura describes as her favorite, involves Laura "playing a puppy and Sarah playing the owner." In the game, "she likes to put me in a pretend cage . . . which is the couch." Laura thinks that Sarah is "a good owner [because] when I start howling and getting really, really sad, she lets me out." Laura says that Sarah's favorite character is Winnie the Pooh and that "she likes to watch the *Book of Pooh* on the Disney channel." Laura proudly announces that her favorite television show is *Scooby Doo*. She "loves" *Scooby Doo* because of "all of the monsters," who don't scare her at all. Laura describes Scooby Doo as a "dog who finds out [about] mysteries with his gang." She especially "likes the way he talks and says scooby doo be doo."

While Laura and Sarah are close, they sometimes have sibling disagreements. For example, Laura describes a time when she and Sarah were playing with Barbie dolls. "We were playing with Mermaid Barbie. We kept fighting over it because we both wanted it. Then we found the other mermaid and that settled it." "They are best friends" is the way Laura's mom describes the relationship between Laura and Sarah. "Sarah is much quieter than Laura, but they get along just great."

Laura speaks with just as much affection when she describes her older sister Courtney. Courtney is in the seventh grade and she likes to "play with us, tickle us, and play tricks on us." Courtney has a best friend who lives next door, who "she talks to a lot on the phone." In fact, according to Mom, Courtney has a good relationship with both Laura and Sarah. "They idolize her. Everything she does, they want to do. She likes *NSYNC, so they like *NSYNC." Mom believes that overall Courtney is great with the girls. However, in the last year or so "she has backed off a bit." As a seventh grader, Courtney has made it clear that she needs some space of her own, especially when her friends are over at the house. Mom believes that both Laura and Sarah will simply have to get used to this change.

Laura also likes to invite her neighborhood friend, Angela, over to her house to play. "We play in the basement and we like to play babies." Laura plays the mother and Angela plays the baby because "she [Angela] really likes to play the baby and I'm a good mommy." A good mommy means that "I tuck her in at night, walk her, and see [watch] her."

Laura has a best friend too. She describes Rose as having "kinda brown skin, short black hair, and about this tall" (pointing to a height significantly above her own). Laura and Rose became friends in kindergarten, where "we got along together, so we became best friends." Rose attends the same elementary school as Laura, and "we sometimes play on the playground at school." At times "she [Rose] runs away from me and that makes me feel bad.

I have to get my friends and my cousin to help me get her back. They're like in second grade." When Rose runs away, Laura will sometimes play with several of her other friends. Laura says that this often causes Rose to "get mad." "When I try to explain to her that I don't like it when she runs away, she backs up and runs again. Sometimes, I just have to leave her alone."

Laura has a large circle of friends and is very popular among the students in her first grade class. Her mom describes her as "very social and . . . always being invited to birthday parties." In fact, her mom believes that one of Laura's greatest strengths is "her people skills. She is awesome . . . and she can get along with anybody. She goes out of her way to be friends with kids. We did have some little friend thing [difficulty], . . . but she seems to be working through it." Her mom goes on to describe her as a "social butterfly." Laura's first grade teacher, Ms. McCarthy, agrees that Laura is very social. Ms. McCarthy says,

> she has a lot of friends and would never single any student out or make any-
> one feel uncomfortable. She never has any negative encounters with other
> students. She would never exclude anyone. For example, when [Laura] is
> playing a game and the game only allows two players, I have heard her say to
> another child who expresses an interest in playing, 'you can play the winner.'
> She is very aware of the feelings of others. She plays with all kids.

This play sometimes even includes boys. In fact, Laura says that she and her friends sometimes "chase boys." When she and her friends catch the boys, which is a source of great pride, they "try to give 'em cooties and then put them in a soup. There is a tire on the playground and we pretend it's the soup."

Her playfulness and outgoing personality spill over into the classroom. Ms. McCarthy feels that Laura is "such a friendly kid," and she expects her to be a class leader. In addition to her strong social skills, Ms. McCarthy believes that Laura will be at the "top of her class." Academically she is an average to high student now. Ms. McCarthy believes that her "reading, writing, and math are very strong. In fact, she can read very well and is in one of the top reading groups." Ms. McCarthy believes that Laura has "no real weaknesses" and says that she is a "wonderful student, is anxious to learn, and a quick learner." Ms. McCarthy describes her as "always motivated and always wanting to do her best." She believes that besides Laura's natural academic abilities, her strong family support and her strong verbal skills contribute to her overall success. Ms. McCarthy points out that Laura "never turns her nose up" at any classroom activity. She is "always ready to work." Ms. McCarthy feels that Laura's strong work ethic comes from the family support she receives. Despite the fact that both parents work full time and Dad does some traveling,

> they are both there for [Laura]. Mom volunteers a lot. She will come on field trips. I can always count on her for support. If something is not right with Laura, [Mom] will give me a heads up.

Ms. McCarthy says that Laura's favorite subject appears to be art. Her enjoyment of art became apparent during a recent classroom activity that involved working on the "wh" sound. Laura decided to draw a picture of a whale. "She put a lot of detail into her whale. That is what she does. If she writes a sentence or a story, she wants to draw a picture and wants to finish it with great detail. Her pictures are remarkable and distinctive." Laura's interest in art is echoed by her mom. "She loves anything having to do with art. She is very good." In addition to art, Laura has demonstrated significant singing talent. In fact, according to Mom, her music teacher has indicated "she has never heard a kindergartener with a voice like hers."

Laura describes some childhood experiences that make her happy, sad, and angry. She, in fact, has a clear idea of the things that she likes and the things she dislikes. For example,

> the things that make me happy is when I get something I want or when people give me surprises or presents. What makes me sad is when Rose runs away from me. And the thing that makes me angry is when somebody takes a toy away from me and they don't give it back. It also makes me sad when people say they don't want to be my friend. Once in kindergarten, Rose said she wouldn't be my friend anymore [the difficulty Laura's Mom was referring to]. I started to cry and went over to my cubby. Then Rose came over and said I'm sorry . . . then I stopped crying and we hugged and were best friends again.

As was the case with many children, and of course even adults, the events of September 11, 2001, evoked many different emotions in Laura. First, Laura describes the events as "planes crashing into buildings because there wasn't any lights on the buildings to tell them where they [the buildings] were." Laura thought about all of the pain and hurt caused by the planes. "I felt bad because when other people get hurt, like when someone is crying, I will follow the crying and ask what is wrong. I was worried that people would get hurt or die."

In addition to the events of September 11, Laura became worried about divorce when the parents of a close friend separated. Laura's mom says "at least once a month" Laura would ask her a question about divorce. For example, once Laura asked, "You [meaning Mom and Dad] would never get divorced, right? And Daddy would never move out of our house." Mom characterizes Laura as being very concerned that this could happen in their home. Both of Laura's parents took time to reassure her that her family would stay together.

Laura's sensitivity is a source of some concern for her mom. Mom is afraid that "it is so easy to break her heart" and it is "very easy to hurt her." She has a "strong desire to please others and really wants everyone to love her." Mom's concern about Laura's sensitivity caused her to make a special request for a particular first grade teacher. She was worried that Laura would have a difficult time with a teacher who was too rigid or harsh. While the school discourages parents from making teacher requests, Laura's parents made a strong case for Laura being placed with Ms. McCarthy.

Another concern voiced by Laura's mom has to do with her small size. Laura is "much smaller than the other kids," something of which Laura is quite aware. In fact, Laura's little sister is beginning to pass her by. Laura's doctors have reassured the family that Laura is just petite. This, however, doesn't keep other children from teasing her because of her size. In fact, in kindergarten teasing about her small size became a bit of an issue for Laura. Laura's kindergarten teacher, Mrs. Doyle, was keenly aware of this situation. One day she decided to create a new class club. The club was called the Little Bodies, Big Brains Club. Mrs. Doyle made Laura the president. Mom says, "I can't tell you what that did for this child [Laura]. Laura's self-confidence was clearly improved by this experience." According to Ms. McCarthy, this self-confidence was clearly evident when Laura arrived in first grade. Her self-confidence is strong and is cultivated in this nurturing classroom, in Laura's home environment, and in other areas of the school community. Recently Laura won the "super kid award." The award was given out by Mr. P., the gym teacher. Mom says that Laura was so excited about this award that she could not wait to share the news with her family and friends. The award is only "given to people who work hard," says Laura and it is given by the "very funny" Mr. P.

While she speaks fondly of Mr. P, her cute nose scrunches up when she talks about her music teacher. "People call her the crazy lady because sometimes it seems like she is going crazy." Despite this characterization of her music teacher, Laura says she likes her because "sometimes she is silly and teaches us the heartbeat."

Laura's ability to perceive what both adults and children think and feel is also evident in her description of Ms. McCarthy. Sometimes "Ms. McCarthy gets funny mad and sometimes she gets real mad." When she gets "really mad she yells, like when kids don't follow directions. I feel sorry for them [when they get yelled at]."

However, her empathy for classmates does not diminish her liking for Ms. McCarthy. The affection felt by Laura toward Ms. McCarthy runs both ways. In fact, it takes Ms. McCarthy only a few words to sum up her opinion of Laura. "She has it all." Laura sums up her feelings for Ms. McCarthy by paying her the ultimate compliment. Even at this very young age, Laura is clear on what she wants to do when she grows up. "I might want to be a dance teacher or just a regular teacher . . . probably first grade."

DISCUSSION QUESTIONS

1. Using evidence from the case, discuss Laura's social cognition. Specifically, address the development of her sense of self, self-perceptions, and her beliefs about relationships as well as the development of her "theory of mind"—her awareness of others' intentions, thoughts, beliefs, and feelings.

2. Agree or disagree with the following: "Laura's parents are excellent parents." Provide support for your position, applying what you have learned about the developmental effects of various parenting practices, environmental factors under the control of parents, and the like to the specifics of Laura's case.

3. Laura's mom describes her as "very social." In fact, her mom believes that one of Laura's greatest strengths is "her people skills. She is awesome . . . and she can get along with anybody. She goes out of her way to be friends with kids." Laura's mom also describes Laura as having a "strong desire to please others" and really wanting "everyone to love her." Discuss the positive and negative effects of such an orientation on Laura's future social and cognitive development. Use research to support your discussion points.

4. Discuss the various social and cognitive developmental effects of Laura's place as the "middle child."

5. Discuss Laura's interactions with Rose. What do they reveal about Laura's development?

6. What if the school administrator refused the request made by Laura's parents for a particular first grade teacher? In what ways would you suggest they deal with a teacher who lacks Ms. McCarthy's warmth and creativity?

APPLYING THEORETICAL PERSPECTIVES

1. Discuss the factors in Laura's life that have contributed, in your opinion, to Ms. McCarthy's assessment of Laura as a child who "has it all." Use evidence from the case and information from your course and various theories of development you have studied to support your opinion.

2. Laura's teacher and her mom talk about her imagination and fantasy play. Discuss the role that these have played in her cognitive development. Use the cognitive development theories of Piaget and Vygotsky to explain your answer.

3. Based on the case, speculate on what Howard Gardner might have to say about Laura.

Also see "Connecting Across Cases" question 1, in the Introduction to this book.

CLASS ACTIVITY

1. Speculate on the "case" Laura's parents may have made for Laura's placement with Ms. McCarthy, and role-play the conversation between them and school administrators.

RESEARCH SUGGESTION

1. Gardner's theory of multiple intelligences has caused psychologists and educators to expand their definition and understanding of intelligence.

Likewise, it has reinforced for some the belief that existing measures of intelligence are only measuring a limited range of abilities, focusing on verbal and mathematical intelligences. Research ways of assessing other types of intelligences, as proposed by Gardner's theory, and/or develop a lesson that might tap one or more of these abilities.

READINGS AND RESOURCES

Piaget, J. (1962). *Play, dreams, and imitation in childhood.* New York: Norton.

An examination of the importance of imitations, play, and dreams to children's movement from sensory motor schemas to conceptual schemas.

Hubbard, J., & Coie, J. D. (n.d.). *Emotional correlates of social competence in children's peer relationships.* Retrieved June 12, 2004, from www.udel .edu/psych/fingerle/article1.htm#Abstract

This article provides an overview of research on children's social competence and friendship problems.

Gardner, H. (1993). *Frames of mind: The theory of multiple intelligences.* New York: Basic Books.

This book provides a basic overview of Gardner's theory of multiple intelligences and its educational implications.

FOUR

EMILY'S WORLD

Nurturing a Child With Autism

———•◦•———

PRIMARY AND SECONDARY ISSUES

Primary Issues:	*Secondary Issues:*
• The nature and wide range of manifestations of autistic disorder	• Theories regarding the causes of autism
• Theory of mind/metacognition	• Operant behavior therapy
• Parenting a child with autism	• Reinforcement as a motivator
• Treatments of autistic disorder	• Developmental effects of having a sibling with disabilities

CASE

Life is incredibly hectic at Emily's house. She is the oldest of three young children who keep their mother constantly busy caring for them in this lovely home in a medium-sized urban community. Their home is in a middle class neighborhood dotted with large old maple trees. The neighborhood has attracted many young families, and on any given sunny day the sidewalks are filled with children running about and playing.

Emily is often found out in her backyard, swinging contentedly on her swing. She is a bright-eyed six-year-old who at around the age of two was diagnosed with autism. Emily has a younger sister, Karen, who is two and a half years old, and a baby brother, Michael, who just turned one. Mom suspected something was not right with Emily from the beginning. "From the minute she was born, she was delayed with everything. She didn't sit up until she was, I think, a year." Although Emily is nonverbal now, her mom describes some early vocalizations. She was able to say things like "mama, dada, kitty, and pooh." She was also able to say "hi and bye" and, at one point, could even begin the "Old McDonald Had a Farm" nursery rhyme. Additionally, Mom indicates that she "could easily retrieve items I asked her for." For example, if Mom asked for her Tigger or Pooh Bear stuffed animals, she would quickly run and get them.

Thus the focus of concern about Emily, at least very early in her development, was on her physical delays. Once she began a regular program of physical therapy, it became apparent that she had some additional special needs. At about 18 months of age, her physical therapy was expanded to include speech therapy and one-on-one time with a special educator. In fact, at one point "we had four different professionals working with her," reports Mom. Recognizing the need for intensive early intervention, the professionals working with Emily suggested placing her in a full-day special education setting. Mom remembers that at first, following some adjustment, Emily thrived in her new school. She started out in the "orange room, where she did great and was happy going to school." The placement was all day, five days a week. When she got a bit older, Emily was moved to the "purple room." Mom describes this move as a difficult one. Her attitude toward school changed, and she was "unhappy and miserable." Mom believes that Emily's dislike of school was in part due to the lack of sufficient structure and the staff's inability or unwillingness to get her to cooperate.

Emily's parents decided to investigate other possibilities. Their local elementary school was reported to have an excellent self-contained special education program. After some serious investigation and reflection, Emily's parents decided to place her in the public elementary school. This school, with an enrollment of 650 students, kindergarten through sixth grade, is one of three magnet schools in the district in which admission is determined by a random lottery following application. Over one half of the school's students are from minority and ethnic groups, and close to half of the school's students are eligible for free or reduced-price lunch. Approximately 20% of the students in Emily's grade level are students with disabilities ranging from mild to severe. Despite the school's diverse population, the school has achieved state standards for mathematics and English language arts for the past four years. Emily was placed in a self-contained class with 11 other children with special needs, with a head teacher and four aides.

Mom tells of going into the school and meeting Emily's new teachers. At that initial visit, Mom recalls trying to prepare the teachers for a very unhappy and uncooperative child. Given Emily's most recent reaction to school, Mom tried to prepare the teachers for "hard times ahead" with Emily. However, Emily surprised everyone. "I started getting notes home from the teacher telling me that Emily was wonderful at school." She "knew her colors, could match some words, and pick out her own name." Mom believes that between some intensive work at home and her experiences in her old school, "she was able to pick up some basic skills."

Mom strongly believes that Emily's receptive skills far exceed her expressive skills. She is able to understand what is being said to her, but has difficulty demonstrating that understanding. Emily's teacher, Ms. Hammond, strongly agrees. "She seems to understand things, but getting her to demonstrate that understanding is often difficult. I think at times she understands some of the things we are doing." Ms. Hammond describes the following as an example. "One day I was reading the book *Three Little Kittens Have Lost Their Mittens* to the class. Following the story, I had an activity where I gave each child a colored mitten. I then hid some of the mittens around the room and [the students] had to find the mitten that matched the color of their mitten. Emily did not get up. She just sat there. I then got her two different colored mittens and asked her to select the one that matched her mitten. She was successful." She knew how to complete the task, but you could not tell by simply observing her independent behavior. Ms. Hammond goes on to describe several other examples of Emily's purposive behaviors. For example, one day the class baked cookies. When they were done, Ms. Hammond remembers "putting them up on a shelf." The shelf was too high for Emily to reach, so she decided to bring another taller child over to the shelf to get the cookies for her.

Ms. Hammond says that Emily's desire for food is an excellent motivator. Recently, however, the teaching staff has been instructed by Emily's parents and psychologist to stop using food as reinforcement. Emily's mom explains that her desire for food and the use of food as a motivator is creating a weight problem in Emily. "She has breakfast here [at home] and her favorite is toaster waffles. I pack her a snack and then it's off to school where she eats another breakfast. She eats lunch at school, has her snack, and then when she gets home she is crying, demanding to eat some more." Emily's food routine is in the process of being changed, at the recommendation of her psychologist. He believes that Emily is using food as a mechanism for control. She would grab food, run around the house with it, and throw a temper tantrum when it was taken away. At his suggestion, this kind of behavior is no longer tolerated. If she wants to eat, she has to sit in her high chair in the kitchen. Despite some initial strong protest, Emily has adapted well to this new routine. There are times when things are so busy in the morning, Mom notes, "that suddenly I will turn around and Emily is sitting in her high chair waiting to be fed!"

Besides her love of food, Emily enjoys listening to music, swinging on her swing, twirling beads, and taking baths or showers. However, she shows little interest in toys. She "won't pick up a toy and play with a toy or anything like that," says Mom. She also loves it when the backyard is filled with people, especially kids. "She will sit on the swing and just watch the kids. That makes her really happy." When she is playing in the backyard, you can often find Emily all "dressed up." She is very much into "frilly and feminine things." She loves to play "dress up," and Mom has cut up some of her old prom dresses to accommodate Emily's desire to play. This desire is also evident in school. Mom explains that at school there is a dress-up corner, and Emily loves playing there.

Emily appears to be happy when her brother and sister come close to her. "She doesn't go to them, but she likes to have them come to her and sit next to her and watch TV." She especially loves being near her brother, and she felt this way from the beginning. When Emily went to visit her baby brother at the hospital, she "came up and held him and she touched him." Her reaction to Mom going to the hospital to have her two siblings was not as positive. In fact, Mom remembers Emily's behavior as being "off" toward her. She "cried a lot" when Mom left for the hospital, appearing confused and frightened by the separation. As far as her sister is concerned, "she can take her or leave her." Karen, who is two and a half, thinks nothing of taking something she wants from Emily. For example, Emily loves to twirl her beads. Sometimes Karen just wants them. She'll go over to Emily, take a bunch of beads, and "hide them in the couch." One day, Karen kept doing this over and over. The frustration started building up in Emily. She started yelling and got angrier and angrier.

Her answer to this problem was to run right over to Karen "and give her a big bite!"

The social relationships she has developed extend beyond her immediate family. Mom says that Emily has a very special relationship with their next-door neighbor, who is a former high school teacher. "He just talks to her and pays her lots of attention. She'll sometimes just stand at the fence waiting for him to talk to her." Emily has also developed a very strong bond with her grandmother and her uncle. Her large extended family has helped Emily and her parents in so many ways. They are a source of support, love, and encouragement. Emily's Mom explains how grateful she is to both her family and her husband's family. Without them, their lives would be much more difficult.

Emily also spends time with a teenage girl who sometimes baby-sits her. Jill lives across the street from Emily and her family. Mom describes Jill as a pretty typical teenager who is just wonderful to Emily. She takes Emily on special outings and always makes time to be kind to her. Emily always smiles when she gets to go over to Jill's house to visit. One day, Mom went into the house for a second to get the baby. Emily was busy on her swing in their fenced-in backyard. The next thing Mom knew, Emily had opened the gate and gone into Jill's backyard to swing on Jill's swing. Up to that point, Emily had not been able to unlock the gate. Now that she can, Mom says, "I'll have to have eyes in the back of my head."

Emily can surprise adults with her initiative to get out on her own. During the first week of school, she was well into a routine. Every day Emily and her classmates would take a rest from 1:30–2:00 P.M., then get their backpacks on, get on the bus, and go home. On one particular Friday, because of a schedule change, the children rested from 1:00–1:30 P.M. and then went to gym during their regular rest time. While the kids were in the gym running around, Emily's teacher noticed she was missing. To her amazement, Emily was nowhere to be found. After a frantic search of the gym, the entire school, and the classroom, Ms. Hammond found Emily on the bus. "She had gone back to the classroom, gotten her coat and was waiting to go home on the bus." Ms. Hammond says that they were all "of course upset about her leaving," but felt that it was quite an accomplishment for Emily. She had figured out "it was the normal time to go home and that was exactly what she was going to do." She was going to stick to her routine, despite the fact that she was on the bus a half hour early.

As for school relationships, Ms. Hammond explains that there is not much interaction between Emily and the rest of the students. Similar to her behavior with her sister and brother, Emily will not approach the other children. "If she interacts with the other kids, it is because they have come up to her. Remember, I have a lot of autistic kids in this class, so there is not a lot of interaction. She really doesn't play with the other kids." Her activities in school include "a lot of tactile work," says Ms. Hammond. For example, she "enjoys playing with beads, shaving cream, and play dough." Ms. Hammond will often put the TV on in the morning when the kids are coming into the room (around 7:30 A.M.). Emily watches the shows, notes Ms. Hammond, "but I'm not sure how much she is paying attention to them. She does like the music that goes along with the shows, and sometimes we give her beads to play with as she watches. But we have to be careful with her because she puts everything into her mouth." While food was the big motivator earlier in the school year, it has now been replaced by beads. Emily's time on task is very short, so when Ms. Hammond wants her to complete a task, she says, "first this, then that." Emily knows exactly what that means. If she finishes her work, she will get to play with the beads.

For the most part, Mom agrees that it is hard to know how much Emily understands about the TV shows she watches or the movies she sees. Mom and Dad monitor closely what she watches at home. They allow her to watch a few select Disney cartoons and *Wheel of Fortune,* which she loves. Mom thinks that the spinning of the wheel is what keeps her attention on the game show. There are certain times when Mom is quite certain that Emily understands what she is watching. For example, in the movie *Winnie the Pooh*, there is a scene where Christopher Robin (a story character) must leave. It is very sad and Emily cries whenever she sees this part of the movie. At some level, Mom believes that she understands the sad feelings Christopher and Pooh are experiencing even though she is not able to explain them.

Communication is one of the major concerns for Emily's parents and Ms. Hammond. Since Emily is nonverbal and does not use sign language, alternate methods of communication have been explored. Sign language just "doesn't work because she won't imitate," says Mom. So recently Emily's parents and teachers have begun to work together, encouraging Emily to use the Picture Exchange Communication System (PECS) to help facilitate her communication skills. Charlop-Christy, Carpenter, LeBlanc, and Kellet (2002) describe PECS as a system that uses basic behavior principles, such as shaping, to teach children to communicate using pictures. The child is taught to use pictures affixed to a magnetic or Velcro® board to communicate, with emphasis on the child being able to initiate communication, respond to questions, and make social comments, such as "I see the ball." However, after four months of work Emily's parents and teachers feel that her lack of real progress in this area does not bode well for future language development. Ms. Hammond says, "I have not seen huge progress this year and I'm not sure I will. I want to get her to the point where she can better communicate using PECS."

As is clearly evident with their collaboration on the PECS system, the interaction between home and school is consistent, supportive, and strong. Ms. Hammond characterizes Emily's parents as "remarkable people." They are very involved in Emily's school activities. It is not unusual for Dad "to take the day off for Halloween just to be with her. Mom volunteers whenever she can. She has two other children at home but is always willing to help out. She sent us [the teachers] this beautiful card at Christmas that she made. I don't know where she finds the time. Emily is a tremendous amount of work and put two kids on top of that. Mom is just amazing. And she is so appreciative for whatever we do with Emily."

Mom and Dad's hopes for Emily are the same as those of any parents of a six-year-old. They want her to be happy and to be as successful as she can be. Knowing when Emily is happy is not always easy. In fact, Mom says that it is sometimes hard to know if she is happy. There are times when "she cries for no apparent reason." This is especially true at bedtime. The family deals with this by having all five of them go into Emily's room together. "That makes her happy." She just doesn't like "to be by herself." Being with her family and hearing compliments on her "pretty clothes" makes her smile.

It is hard to define what success will mean for Emily. Mom says that she "must be pushed" to do things or she would be content to just sit around. However, all who are concerned with Emily's future know that sitting around will not advance her development. Despite the frustrations associated with caring for and finding the right care for Emily, her parents are committed to the struggle. In fact, not only her parents but extended family, friends, and teachers are trying to provide that loving "push" to help maximize her developmental progress.

DISCUSSION QUESTIONS

1. Describe characteristics exhibited by Emily that are "typical" in autistic disorder as originally described by Leo Kanner. Describe characteristics

that are "atypical" of Kanner's description. Be specific, using details from the case.

2. Some theorists contend that cognitive and social aspects of autism may be related to a deficiency in metacognition or lack of "a theory of mind"—that persons with autism "seem unable to understand that mental states such as knowledge, beliefs, and expectations exist and are connected to people's behavior" (Hetherington & Parke, 2003, p. 697). Others theorize that autistic children have either an undersensitivity or oversensitivity to sensory stimulation, and therefore behaviors such as social withdrawal and the desire for a predictable environment help to make the world more tolerable. Discuss how Emily's observed behaviors and competencies (or lack thereof) support or fail to support these theories.

3. How did Emily's teachers address her special needs in their activities and structuring of the classroom environment? Create a lesson and explain how you would set it up to maximize the likelihood that Emily could complete it successfully. Support your answer with information from the text.

4. In what ways did Emily's parents and teachers help her to achieve the optimal level of development? Why is active intervention essential when working with a child with autism?

APPLYING THEORETICAL PERSPECTIVES

1. Describe the process of operant conditioning and how it was used in Emily's case either intentionally or unintentionally. You should be specific, incorporating your knowledge of operant conditioning and your knowledge of Emily based on the case. How would you use behavior learning theorists' terms to describe how Emily's parents discontinued the use of food as a reinforcer?

2. Using Bronfenbrenner's ecological systems theory, speculate about Emily's effect on her family system, paying particular attention to her siblings. For example, consider her siblings and how the presence of Emily as a disabled child within their microsystems might influence their socialization and emotional development. How might Emily's

presence influence the way her siblings react to cultural values in their macrosystems? How might the effects on Emily's parents and extended family consequently affect her siblings? Speculate with regard to all systems described by Bronfenbrenner, including the chronosystem.

CLASS ACTIVITY

1. Design a lesson for a child with autism, such as Emily, that takes into consideration her limited communication skills. Present your lesson to the class.

RESEARCH SUGGESTIONS

1. Autistic disorder is now understood as more of a "spectrum" disorder. Research what the term "spectrum disorder" means and how Emily might be classified within the spectrum of autism today. Defend your classification based on what you know about Emily.

2. Research the Picture Exchange Communication System and describe its various uses, advantages, and disadvantages from a developmental perspective.

3. Although autism usually involves impaired communication and social abilities, Emily appears to enjoy and seek out social contact. What does research suggest as possible explanations for this behavior?

READINGS AND RESOURCES

Autism Society of America at www.autism-society.org

The Autism Society of America is a parent-led organization that provides information about autism and advocacy for persons with autism.

Special Needs Families Resource Center at www.specialfamilies.com

This Web site provides resources and support to families with children with autism.

Bondy, A., & Frost, L. (1994). The picture exchange communication system. *Focus on Autistic Behavior, 9,* 1–19.

This article provides an overview of PECS as an effective method of communication for children with autism and other developmental disabilities.

Iowannone, R., Dunlap, G., Huber, H., & Kincaid, D. (2003). Effective educational practices for students with autism spectrum disorders. *Focus on Autism and Other Developmental Disabilities, 18*(3), 150–165.

This article describes the key elements that should be included in a comprehensive instructional program for children with ASD. All elements are supported by sound empirical research.

FIVE

NICOLE AND BROOKE

Homeschooled Fraternal Twins

PRIMARY AND SECONDARY ISSUES

Primary Issues:	*Secondary Issues:*
• Sociocultural influences on cognitive development	• Attachment
	• Early physical development
• Twins and sibling relationships	• Personality and temperament
	• Learning styles
• Homeschooling	• Friendship
• Nature versus nurture	

CASE

Nicole and Brooke are nine-year-old fraternal twins, but right from the start they were different. Brooke was born first and weighed 7 pounds and 11 ounces. Her father says that she was "pink, alert, and crying. She was ready and on the go. She looked like the Gerber baby." Due to complications, Nicole was born 10 minutes later. She weighed a little less than 5 pounds, was limp and not breathing. She had an initial Apgar score of 2. If the birth had been a vaginal delivery, their mother said, "Nicole would have come out first. She was further down. But because it was a caesarean, Brooke popped up first." As Nicole recounts the story, "I couldn't breathe when I was a baby, but Brooke, she could really scream. She was like the loudest baby in the hospital. Mom did a special surgery that made Brooke older, but if they just did the regular . . . then I would have been the oldest."

Nicole was resuscitated and made a quick recovery; her second Apgar was 9. However, Brooke continued to develop physically faster than Nicole. Nicole walked five months later than Brooke, was toilet trained later, and did not develop her first tooth until 17 months of age. The family doctors reassured their parents that both girls were developing normally with no serious problems, in part because Nicole always caught up to Brooke very quickly. Dad points out that although Brooke's motor development was early and steady, when "Nicole started walking, it was like overnight." Similarly, he thought that Nicole could have mastered toilet training earlier, but "she just didn't feel like going." Dad says he sometimes wonders, "If Nicole had come first would we have dealt with them differently?" However, he believes that they "would have treated Brooke as the oldest, regardless of when she came," due to the differences in physical development.

Temperamental differences between the girls were also apparent very early, says Dad. "Nicole seems to be more laid back, but when she wants something, she makes it known. When they were first born, the very next day I went to the hospital. . . . This was like 12 hours after birth, and the nurse came up to me and said, 'Man, she's stubborn' [because she wouldn't take the bottle]. I kinda looked at her and said, 'It's 12 hours?'" However, Nicole's strong nature came through in her refusals to always give in to Brooke in their early play together. As Dad describes, "There'd be eight or nine toys they'd be playing with, and every toy Nicole would pick up, Brooke would take, and Nicole could care less 'cause Brooke had to have every toy. . . . Finally Nicole would pick up something and Brooke would take it. And Nicole would take it back. And Brooke would take it, and Nicole would take it back. In other words, that's the one toy Nicole wanted."

In contrast to Nicole, Mom describes Brooke as "very active, very busy. She's always doing a lot of things at once. . . . Nicole can lay and watch TV for three hours. Brooke could not. She can watch TV, but she's gotta be doing everything else at the same time." Her parents describe her as "driven" to excel in everything she does, and they worry that she is sometimes too hard on herself.

Mom tells her, "I'm afraid you're gonna forget to have your babies, you know she's so busy all the time." Brooke usually completes her work faster than Nicole, but makes mistakes because of her impulsiveness and eagerness to move on. Brooke is also very athletic and enjoys playing sports like basketball with boys. She enjoys the competitive nature of sports and the rough and tumble play of the boys. Her father says that she is "almost like a boy in some ways" and remembers that she actually wanted to wear a bow tie to nursery school. Her mother says Brooke is sometimes "overly honest" with people, saying things before she considers how the other person might react.

Their parents say that Nicole is more meticulous than Brooke and likes to take her time. She is a "deep thinker" who reflects on problems rather than jumping to a solution. Nicole also prefers "frilly things" and likes wearing dresses. "Nicole's strength is she is just so sweet," says Mom. "Kids always like her because she's just so easy to get along with. . . . she can be with anybody and she doesn't want to take the lead." Mom worries that Nicole might just "let life pass her by and daydream," or that she will have difficulty separating from Brooke. Nicole describes herself as quiet and shy, pointing out that she only talked to one person on the first day of preschool. Her mother agrees that she is "painfully, painfully shy on certain things and if she's on stage, she freezes." In a recent relay race, Nicole was much slower than other children, not because her physical development was deficient, but because she was worried about other people watching her. Nicole prefers activities where she is not the focus of attention and always looks for ways to help others. Nicole says that "my mom usually gets me things because I don't ask for too much, while Brooke on the other hand, she probably asks for a lot of things." Mom emphasizes that the twins look out for each other and usually insist on splitting everything. "Brooke wanted to buy a ring a couple of weeks ago, but she didn't want to spend the money. So Nicole gave her some of her money to buy the ring."

However, Nicole has a mischievous side that was apparent early on. She would do things to get reactions from Brooke, such as crying out, "Eh!" or snapping the front closure of the stroller on Brooke's side. When Brooke acted startled or cried out, Nicole would giggle. In kindergarten, she again showed herself capable of impressive deception. She came home from kindergarten one day and said, "The school nurse told me I got to lay on the couch today and watch TV 'cause I'm not feeling well." Her mother went to the school the next day, angry because they did not call to tell her Nicole was sick. The school nurse told her she had not seen Nicole the day before. "So I look down at Nicole and I hear, 'Uh-oh.'" Mom said she realized that Brooke had gone home the day before with broken glasses, and Nicole was trying to bring attention to herself.

Overall, their parents describe the twins as "extremely close. They're each other's best friend." Dad points out that "they'll get on each other's nerves a lot 'cause they spend so much time together." However, they are rarely apart and refuse to sleep in separate rooms although their house has two extra bedrooms. Sometimes, Mom says, they use their differences to help each other out. "Like when they started to wear a bra. Brooke is too busy to figure out the whole bra bit, so she's gotta have Nicole help with that. . . . Even though Nicole is like the younger sister when it comes to certain things, Brooke really needs her." Another time, Brooke forgot to wear her boots to kindergarten, and Nicole shared one of her boots so that each girl went home with one shoe and one boot.

Despite their differences, both girls are conscientious and intelligent. They share an interest in science, although Brooke's strength is in memorizing facts while Nicole likes to do scientific drawings. They both enjoy swimming and briefly took ballet dancing together until they were "thrown out of class" because Brooke kept carrying Nicole around the room. Dad says, "They have interests that are similar, but even in their similarities, they're beginning to look at differences." They used to dress alike, but now Brooke doesn't want to dress the same and complains that Nicole sometimes "copies" her. Nicole shows an interest in sharing clothes with Brooke, but admits that Brooke wants her own clothes.

Brooke says she likes being a twin. "Sometimes when you read books about it . . . you feel happy . . . that it happened to you and everything. It's also a playmate sometimes 'cause you can do all the same things." Nicole says that an advantage of being a twin is that she and Brooke are usually included together in many activities and parties. She describes Brooke as "my first best friend." Recognizing how close the twins were, their parents requested that they be placed in the same classroom in their first years of nursery and elementary school. When they were separated in kindergarten, they found ways to talk to each other through a "milk closet" that connected the two rooms. Brooke or Nicole would go into the room to get the snacks and "wait until the other one would come for her milk." Other students also treated them "as a unit," expecting them to choose each other for activities that required pairing. The strength of their identity as twins is especially striking because the girls differ so much in their physical appearance. Brooke is taller, with thick curly blond hair and bright, lively blue eyes. She is constantly moving and talking, inquiring about everything she encounters. Nicole is smaller and dark haired, with dark brown eyes that linger and look deeply into the faces of others. She often sits back, quietly observing others, but can surprise you with her memory for details that she takes in.

Nicole and Brooke share a room with their cat, Angel, in their family's four-bedroom house on a quiet suburban street in upstate New York. Their family got Angel and a litter mate, Tabby, when the girls were two years old. Brooke speaks sadly of how Tabby died of FIP within six months. "She wasn't even half a year old when she died . . . that's sad 'cause she was just little. She used to take care of Angel. She used to bathe her and everything." Both girls are fond of Angel although they have different ideas about how she should be treated. Nicole likes to play with Angel because she is "fun." She says that the cat sleeps under her bed but sits on Brooke's bed. Brooke says that Angel is afraid to jump on Nicole's bed because "she is always fussing over the cat." Brooke says that the cat will come to her when she calls it more readily than to anyone else in the family. "She comes over and I usually pet her or something. Nicole would usually pick her up and then [pause] one time she pretends like she was a baby . . . and she grabs a towel and she stuffs Angel in the towel, wraps it around her." Brooke laughs and says, "Angel really didn't like that." Nicole says that she sometimes tells Angel what she is thinking or feeling because "[Angel] can't tell secrets. She might say to me a meow, but no one will understand." The girls would like to have more animals, but their parents have said they must wait until they are older and can take responsibility for them. Meanwhile, they have filled their room with stuffed animals of all kinds.

While Brooke and Nicole both love animals, they often pursue different interests and activities. Both profess a love of television and enjoy watching the Cartoon Network, Disney Channel, and Nickelodeon. Nicole likes a show called *As Told by Ginger,* about youth trying to survive junior high school. She also likes Reggie in *Rocket Power* because "she's kind of like [pause] a leader. . . . She's not really the leader, but she's nice and friendly." Brooke's favorite shows are *Scooby Doo* and *ER.* She can name most of the main characters on *ER* and says that she likes it because "you never know what's going to happen—suspense, drama. And . . . something that's interesting about it. . . . You might even have to watch the other episode to find out what's going to happen." While the girls enjoy many of the same shows, they sometimes argue over what to watch. Their parents limit television watching during the week, and if the girls can't agree on what to watch, they sometimes ask their parents to make the final choice. As Brooke says, "I don't care what it is. Let's just watch something."

Brooke loves computer games, basketball, and soccer, while Nicole enjoys art and gymnastics. Brooke says that Nicole's "relaxed" manner sometimes makes it hard to play together since she likes more active pursuits and Nicole likes to "daydream." Nicole's favorite games usually involve some type of pretending. She and Brooke sometimes pretend that they are on an adventure in Alaska or Egypt. With friends, they like to make up stories and pretend they are characters in their favorite television shows or movies, such as *Jurassic Park 4* or *As Told by Ginger.* This year, for the first time, Nicole and Brooke also chose different Halloween costumes. Brooke is dressing as a sports hero and Nicole is going as a witch.

Many of the girls' activities are planned by their parents, in part because the family has been homeschooling for the last two years. Both parents work flexible jobs that allow them to make time to teach the girls from home. Dad is a consultant for the state department of education and teaches part-time at a local college. He loves to tell stories about his daughters, enhanced by his animated reenactments of their facial expressions, verbal comments, and gestures. He has the dark hair and eyes characteristic of his Puerto Rican heritage and amuses friends with his detailed stories and ability to deliver humorous tales with a straight face. Since his multiple jobs are demanding, he works energetically and likes to get things right the first time but manages to find time for lunchtime basketball. Mom is a medical researcher who works part-time in a laboratory and provides technical assistance to other research centers. She is a sensitive and caring person who is always looking out for others. Her clients appreciate her meticulous and well-organized approach to solving their problems, and Dad says that it is his wife who also keeps their active household in impeccable order. With her long blond hair and bright blue eyes, she presents a striking visual complement to her husband. Both parents put family needs first when they plan their schedules and activities. They chose a family-oriented neighborhood in which to live and are actively involved in their local church. "We rarely do anything without the girls," says Mom.

Homeschooling allows the girls to spend at least six hours a day with each other and with their mother or father. Nicole says that she felt sad when she went to school because she missed her mother, father, and cat and did not like some of the "mean ladies" in the lunchroom. She also found school confusing because of rules about where you had to put your coat or foods you couldn't eat, like bubble gum. She finds homeschooling more comfortable because she does not have to worry about the scary things that happened to her at school, such as having a stomachache on the bus or getting locked out of school after recess. She does remember fun times at school, in particular some art activities with her favorite teacher. But she likes homeschooling better because "I'm not alone, but I'm not that like crowded up with people." She also likes not "wasting" time riding the bus, and she thinks her mom and dad are "not as strict" as some of her teachers were.

Brooke says that the best thing about homeschooling is she doesn't have to wait for all the other kids to get done with their work, and they usually get done with school earlier. "When in school, they might just keep throwing work at you 'cause then the buses aren't going to leave just for you." She says she still has to wait for Nicole to finish, though. "Sometimes I start like 10, 20 minutes later . . . so to give her a head start, but I always get caught up with her." Dad admits that when he gives the girls an assignment and checks back "20 minutes, 30 minutes later, Brooke is pretty much fairly done, and Nicole is on the third problem." But Mom says, "It's not that Nicole can't; she's just busy looking out the window." In fact, she says when they first started homeschooling, they considered Nicole's daydreaming tendencies in arranging the desks in their room. "We said, 'if we catch you looking out the window too much, you're going against the wall.'"

Mom says that she found "letting go" very difficult when the girls first went to kindergarten and were placed in different classrooms because the school did not believe in putting siblings together. She and her husband both helped out frequently in the kindergarten classrooms and then requested that the girls be put into the same first grade room. The principal resisted, citing research showing negative effects due to sibling competition. However, Dad said, "We know our daughters. They're not competitive, they are complementary to each other. . . . They have their own distinct individualities; they help each other out more than they compete with each other." The principal finally allowed them to be placed together for first grade, but said he could not promise the same would happen in later grades. Both parents said they continued to volunteer in the first grade classroom, but found they were usually helping "kids who needed extra help" and not their daughters. They were also concerned that the teachers in the higher grades did not seem to "want [parents] to volunteer." They began to consider homeschooling as a serious option after one of their friends decided to homeschool her five sons. On the day after the shootings at Columbine High School, they presented the home-schooling option to Brooke and Nicole, and they agreed that they wanted to try it. Mom admits that initially the "real reason" for homeschooling "was 'cause I wanted them home with me." However, now both parents believe that the academic advantages of being able to maximize the girls' potentials by work-ing in a more individualized manner are equally important.

Mom works with the girls two days a week on science, art, reading, and writing, while Dad covers math, geography, and history on the other three days. Dad is also teaching both girls to speak Spanish. The school day usually begins at 7:30 and lasts until 1:30 or 2:00, but Brooke says that Mom and Dad have different approaches. Dad makes them do homework "right after we do school. Our mom's homework is usually later at night, like after dinner." They work in a variety of places: the living room, kitchen, Mom's office, their bedrooms, or even outside. Sometimes they work at the local library or do a "Barnes and Noble day" when they go to the bookstore and spend the day reading books of their own choice. The whole family sometimes takes a field trip to the state museum, an educational center such as a nearby geological park with caves, or a historical site such as a Revolutionary War battlefield. Recently they all accompanied Mom on a business trip to Boston, and Dad and the girls toured the city while their mother worked. Dad enjoys making learning practical and relating it to the real world. He frequently uses Mom's business trips to prompt the girls' interest in learning geography.

Their parents use supplemental curricula, which provide packets of mate-rials and activities. One of Brooke's favorite activities is working on the human body, while Nicole enjoys art and math. Their parents customize their teaching to the girls' strengths and watch out for their weaknesses. They say that both girls score in the high 90th percentiles on the California Achievement Tests, but they make very different types of mistakes on their tests. Brooke is very good in science and has an exceptional memory, while Nicole excels at math and writing. Dad points out that Brooke can tell you about the functions of every body part and name all the capitals of the 46 countries in Europe. She is fast in getting her work done and eager to move on to the next assignment. Mom says, "Brooke just wants to get it done right now, whereas Nicole will spend the time. In September they were doing a ghost story, and by the end of two weeks I said, 'Nicole, you got to end that story at some point,' 'cause she would just go on and on and on." Similarly in Spanish, Dad says that "Nicole's very good, not that she knew Spanish, but she's much stronger than Brooke because she'll take her time." However, he does have to remind Nicole to pay attention to the details. On one recent test, Nicole missed two problems because she didn't reduce the fractions despite her father's reminder to do so. "I said, 'Nicole, you know the stuff, you got the right answer, you just got to remember to put it in the simplest terms.'" Both girls hate to get anything wrong and sometimes plead to retake their tests. They also help each other with their work, so their complementary interests and abilities provide them with additional support. Their major concerns, according to Dad, are to stay equal in their work so that they can continue to work together. "Brooke isn't the competition. It's like, Brooke is here [motions at a certain height] so [Nicole] would like to be up here [motions to the same height]. . . . not because she wanted to be better, but because she wanted to be with her." If Nicole does not do as well as her sister, Brooke encourages her, "Nicole, you can do this!"

Dad uses his knowledge of his daughters to tailor lessons to their interests. When the Olympics were in Australia, he made that the focus of their geography lessons and incorporated koala bears (one of their favorite animals) into it as well. Since both enjoy computer games, he also uses "Carmen Sandiego" as a teaching tool. When they studied the history of Greece, the girls showed an interest in mythology so he expanded their reading of the ancient Greek myths. Mom uses projects in both science and art and says that although the girls help each other out, they usually "each do their own type of thing." They get a lot of ideas for projects from an enrichment program that the girls attend on Saturdays at a local college. The girls also take part in other afterschool activities, such as 4H, piano lessons, gymnastics for Nicole, and a basketball team for Brooke.

Their parents say that the girls are getting more self-directed as they get older and often check their own work now. They are also more sophisticated, and Mom says that they find a lot of information on their own. "They read the encyclopedias. Sometimes they just sit there and read, and they do a lot on the computer." She feels that they may soon need more challenge in some subject areas. The parents hired a tutor for art this year because Mom felt that she was not challenging the girls enough. She says that although she thinks she could teach chemistry and Dad could teach physics, they may have to hire tutors for other areas, such as biology.

Although their parents ask them repeatedly if they want to return to the regular school, both girls say that they want to continue homeschooling.

Brooke admits that fourth grade is harder than third grade, but she still likes learning at home. Nicole agrees and says, "I like being with Brooke. . . . If I'm in the regular school, Brooke and I could be in different classes." She wants homeschooling to continue "up to college, and then when we go to college . . . I'm going to go to my dad's college." She admits that her mother's offer to buy her a car if she goes to her husband's college (where the girls would get a tuition discount) is an incentive.

The girls value their close family, but also have friends in several different settings. Nicole says that she plays with several friends in the neighborhood who are her age or a little older. Brooke has one close neighborhood friend, Brianne, but says that most of her friends live several miles away, and she relies on her parents to drive her to their houses. Both girls play with a 10-year-old girl, Karen, who lives down the street, but complain that she can be "bossy." Karen sometimes sets her own rules or just tells them how to play a game. Then both Nicole and Brooke tell her she is not being fair. As Brooke points out, the outcome varies: "Sometimes we get into a fight. Sometimes she just leaves. Sometimes we work things out. Sometimes we just play along maybe." Nicole says that Karen has been getting better and has twice invited them to her pool. However, she says, "the nicer that she gets, but now, it's kind of like she doesn't really spend much time with us." Nicole's "second best friend" after Brooke is Emily, whom she met in first grade. While they no longer attend school together, the girls still visit each other's houses and see each other at parties. Nicole also sees two other first grade friends, Sue Marie and Stacey, and says the only things she misses about her old school are the parties with her friends.

Mom and Dad work with other families who are homeschooling to make sure the girls have many opportunities for play and social activities. Once a week they "switch" with another family that is homeschooling its five boys aged 4, 6, 7, 9, and 10 years. Mom says, "I wanted the girls to be separated at times, so I drop one of the girls off and pick up one of the boys to play with the other girl here." Brooke especially enjoys playing football, basketball, and soccer with the boys, although she says that they "sometimes get into arguments with each other. I just stay out of it then." One of the boys helped her to get over a fear of the basketball that she had developed after she got hit in the nose.

Brooke and Nicole both have friends at their family's "camp" on a lake near a small town in the Catskills. Their family spends much of the summer and frequent weekends during the spring and fall at the camp. The girls enjoy catching frogs, swimming, playing Spud, and watching movies with the children in two nearby families. One family includes two girls and one boy. Another 12-year-old friend, Andi, lives on the lake during the summer and has invited them to visit at her home on Long Island.

Nicole and Brooke are also close to members of their extended family. Their grandparents (on Dad's side) sometimes visit the family camp, and the girls have visited their grandparents at their home in Puerto Rico. The girls especially enjoy spending weekends with their Aunt Katie in a nearby town. Mom admits that Aunt Katie "dotes" on the girls, frequently treating them to trips to the movies, ice cream, and activities such as miniature golf. The girls emphasize that they really enjoy doing things with their family and feel that they do things equally with both parents and with each other.

As they look toward the future, both girls are considering careers that reflect their talents, interests, and family values. Brooke is planning to be a doctor and notes that she won an award in a science fair in third grade. She also would like to write research books on nature. Nicole says she "wants to be about five or six things. An illustrator, an artist, a veterinarian . . . and someone who works at an animal shelter . . . and a singer, like Britney Spears." She would like to illustrate children's books on animals or adventure, but says she won't settle for just one career. "I'm gonna try to do five of them. But first I'll . . . take a class for veterinarians because that will probably cost the most money and also take the longest. Then I'm probably gonna do the artist, then I'm probably gonna do the singing chorus stuff.

Their parents have many dreams and worries about the girls. Dad says that he sometimes thinks, "Wouldn't it be great if they went to Harvard on an academic and athletic or esthetic type of scholarship . . . but my bigger dream is to see them stay the way they are, you know, grow up as adults, but still, I like the way they are now. I wish 15 years from now they're the same way." Mom worries that a medical career would be hard on Brooke, who is already very sensitive about getting anything wrong. Mom says, "I try to talk her out of the medical field. I keep saying maybe you should be a nurse because she's so driven." On the other hand, she worries that Nicole will "go along with Brooke and she won't develop on her own. She doesn't have the drive, so she might be a Mom eating bon-bons all day . . . and wasting her life, 'cause she is smart, but she's okay to just let life pass her by and daydream." However, both parents say that their strongest dream for the girls is "to be whatever they want to be and that they're happy." Dad also expresses concerns about his daughters' safety and well-being. "You hope you can sort of protect them from any type of hurt, and it's probably beyond you, but I keep saying, you know, they've had nine good years."

Brooke and Nicole also recognize that the world can be a dangerous place. The attack on the World Trade Center frightened both girls. Nicole said, "I was kind of scared because it could have happened anywhere. . . . I felt scared . . . and sad for two reasons, because our friends live in New York City, but actually we found out that they're okay. . . . I felt sad for the other people and other families." Brooke said she talked with her parents about the attack because she wanted to know "why there are enemies out there, why they want to hurt us, and why they would do something like that." However, she said, "It's still big news, but it's past now. There's war and everything, but . . . you just got to move on to other things."

DISCUSSION QUESTIONS

1. Identify aspects of Brooke and Nicole's development that you think are most influenced by either nature or nurture. Be sure to cite information from the case or research from your course to back up your analysis.

2. Discuss the birth and early physical development of Brooke and Nicole using information from your course or research to explain what the Apgar score showed and whether their early physical differences may have long-term effects on their development.

3. How would you characterize the attachment bond between the twins and their parents? What effect is this likely to have on their later social development?

4. Behavioral geneticists point out that all children are influenced by inherited genes, shared environments, and nonshared environments. Discuss how each of these factors might influence the development of Brooke and Nicole. Support your analysis with information from the case and information from your course.

5. What personality and temperamental differences do you see between Brooke and Nicole? What are the likely sources of these differences?

6. Describe how Brooke and Nicole interact as siblings, and indicate how being a twin and being homeschooled might influence the nature of this relationship.

7. How do the friendships that Brooke and Nicole have differ from those of children who are in schools? How might this affect their social development?

8. What approaches to learning do Brooke and Nicole's parents take in their homeschooling? How is this likely to affect the girls' development?

APPLYING THEORETICAL PERSPECTIVES

1. Using a sociocultural perspective, discuss how the learning that occurs in the twins' homeschooling differs from that in a school-based classroom. Use some of the following terms from Vygotsky in your analysis: apprenticeship, mediated learning experience, scaffolding, zone of proximal development.

Also see "Connecting Across Cases" questions 4 and 9, in the Introduction to this book.

CLASS ACTIVITIES

1. Design lessons for Brooke and for Nicole that take into account their different strengths, interests, and learning styles. Present your lesson to the class.

2. Role-play a conversation between Brooke and Nicole and their parents about whether to continue homeschooling for the middle school grades.

RESEARCH SUGGESTIONS

1. Research the development of twins and report to the class on how being a twin affects a child's development. Point out ways in which Brooke and Nicole describe experiences common to twins.

2. Conduct a group research project on the topic of homeschooling. Have members of your group report their findings on the following:

- changes in the number of children homeschooled and reasons for homeschooling
- differences between the families of homeschooled and school-educated children
- academic achievement of homeschoolers versus school-educated children
- social development of homeschoolers versus school-educated children
- legal requirements regarding homeschooling and support systems for homeschooling families

READINGS AND RESOURCES

American Home School Association at www.americanhomeschoolassociation. org

This Web site, sponsored by *Home Education Magazine,* provides general information about homeschooling as well as links to resources for home-schooling families.

Center for the Study of Multiple Births at www.multiplebirth.com

This center is affiliated with the Department of Obstetrics and Gynecology, Northwestern University Medical School and The Prentice Women's Hospital and Maternity Center, Chicago, Illinois. Its Web site provides statistics on twins and articles summarizing research on twin births.

Lines, P. M. (2001). *Homeschooling.* Eugene, OR: ERIC Clearinghouse on Educational Management. (ERIC Document Reproduction No. ED457539)

This ERIC Digest provides practical advice for homeschooling parents and children about legal issues, resources for homeschoolers, college admission procedures, and research on the development of children who are homeschooled.

Rudner, L. M. (1999). Scholastic achievement and demographic characteristics of homeschooled students in 1998. *Education Policy Analysis Archives, 7*(8). Retrieved April 20, 2004, from http://epaa.asu.edu/epaa/v7n8/

This article reports the results of a study of the family backgrounds and educational achievement of over 11,000 homeschooled children.

Welner, K. M., & Welner, K. G. (1999). Contextualizing homeschool data: A response to Rudner. *Education Policy Analysis Archives, 7*(13). Retrieved April 20, 2004, from http://epaa.asu.edu/epaa/v7n13/

This article raises questions about the research methods and issues present in the Rudner article.

SIX

BETH

Finding Her Strengths

————⊷•◆•⊷————

PRIMARY AND SECONDARY ISSUES

Primary Issues:	*Secondary Issues:*
• Cognitive development	• Moral development
• Academic difficulties	• Teacher/parental expectations
• Self-concept/self-esteem	• The effects of birth order on
• Industry vs. inferiority	development, sibling relationships
	• Presence of a stable, caring adult figure
	• Friendship, peer acceptance

CASE

"Four girls, one boy, one cat, and Mom and Dad," is the way Beth describes her family. "I'm closest to my cat and my big sister Sally." Beth, who is 11, is right in the middle of her evenly spaced older and younger siblings. She has two teenage older sisters, Sally and Ann, who are in high school. Phil is Beth's younger brother and Mary is the baby in the family. This religious family lives in a nicely maintained house in an urban community of about 100,000 people.

All the children in the family currently attend public school, although for a few years Beth attended a Catholic school.

Beth loves to talk about her cat and clearly has a special relationship with her. She jumps down from the chair to give her some attention. "Whenever I'm sick, she always comes up and cuddles with me," Beth says as she lovingly pets her cat. The cat is not by any means her only source of comfort. She also talks about her oldest sister Sally as always being around when she needs her. "When I'm sick, she always says, 'I hope you feel better,' and then gets me some ginger ale." Beth says that she feels close to Sally despite the six-year difference in age. Sally, who is finishing her senior year of high school, makes special time for Beth. They often play games and go to the movies together. Beth says her sister Sally "is so nice, and fun, and not mean to me." She loves when her big sister gets to baby-sit for the younger children in the family. "She doesn't slap us around and she doesn't say, 'do this' or 'do that.' She won't say, 'go brush your teeth,' but will say, 'please brush your teeth.'" Sally is apply-ing to colleges and trying to decide if she should stay home or go away to school. If Beth has her way, Sally will go to a local college and live at home. When asked why she wants Sally to stay home, Beth says, "'Cause she is so fun to play with, always nice to me, and always gets me good presents."

Beth has another older sister, 14-year-old Ann. "I don't like her. She is always snotty," says Beth. It seems that most of their disagreements center on the use of the computer and the telephone. According to Beth, Ann tries to dominate these sources of communication. Beth doesn't like this one bit and is quick to say so. Beth looks around to see if Ann is close by. When she real-izes that she's not, she whispers, "Sometimes she acts bad and acts like she is weird. She does that a lot and gets it from her friends. I can tell you that now 'cause she's gone. I wouldn't want to hurt her feelings."

Beth, who shares a room with her younger brother and younger sister, starts out talking about her only brother Phil by laughing. She is very cog-nizant of the fact that he is the only boy in a family of four girls. "There are no boys, except for Dad," she says, conveying some pity for Phil. But she is quick to point out that "he always likes to hurt me, and I don't like it." Phil is just a year and a half younger than Beth, and they spend lots of time together. Mom says that their relationship is "love-hate." They are either "loving each other to death or hating each other."

Her admiration for her younger sister Mary is apparent when Beth describes her. "She loves to play with me and have fun!" Beth clearly likes being the older sister. She says, "I can boss her around," since Mary is the little sister. Beth loves to be Mary's babysitter. She often asks to baby-sit for her and will read her books and play games with her. One thing she especially likes to do with Mary is play school. Beth is always the teacher, and Mary is the student. Usually Mary will cooperate, but some days she does not feel like playing. Beth has little tolerance for this. She will say, "I am the big sister" and "what do you mean you don't want to play?" However, she tries to include games that Mary likes to entice her to play, and she really wants her to have fun. Mom says that on most days you can find them happily playing together.

Beth shares a bedroom with her younger brother and sister, but this doesn't seem to really bother Beth. "Yeah 'cause it's kind of, not scary, because it's fun sharing a bedroom . . . it can be bad because sometimes they sing, and I don't like that." The one part of sharing a bedroom that appears to annoy Beth is that "I never get any time to be by myself in my room 'cause of Phil and Mary." When describing what's good about sharing a bedroom, Beth says that they can talk to each other and they don't feel lonely. The bedroom is small for three children, but each has his or her own bed with toys, posters, and books reflecting his or her personality.

Beth describes her neighborhood as filled with boys. Her house sits in the middle of a city block, surrounded by homes on both sides of the street. She characterizes this as "not good 'cause there's not a lot of girls to play with." She apparently doesn't let this bother her too much. She's often outside playing football with the boys or riding her scooter up and down the block.

Beth's dad works for a governmental agency and her mom works part-time outside the home as a substitute nurse. Her position is in a school for disabled children. Beth's parents share similar values and have similar interests. They enjoy the outdoors, particularly running, and they enjoy spending time with family. They are also active in their church. The family is close-knit, and both parents express much caring and support for each other and their children.

Mom describes Beth as the "middle child . . . with a high activity level." She is very busy "from the moment she gets up until she goes to sleep," says Mom. She loves to be around people and really loves animals. In fact, she has developed a special connection with her Aunt Mary who also loves animals and is into organic farming. Beth spends some time at her aunt's house during the summer. Her aunt lives in a different state, so her trips there occur mostly during the summer. She also has a special bond with her grandparents, who have a summer camp that she visits during her school holidays. Her mom believes that Beth's cheery nature and positive disposition have helped her develop these close relationships with her extended family.

Her love of animals extends beyond her own cat. Beth often goes to the local pet store to buy treats for the neighborhood dogs. Beth reports that she uses her own money for the treats and runs home to give the dogs their biscuits. Mom and Beth describe a time when they talked about going into the dog biscuit business. With a new recipe in hand, they're talking about making their own biscuits. Since Beth also loves to do arts and crafts, she will likely be in charge of designing the logo for the new business.

Beth's caring nature was evident on the days following the September 11 terrorist attacks. She wanted to do something to help, so she and a friend went out and collected money for the Red Cross. Mom indicates "she was obsessed from morning 'til night, and she wanted to do it every day." Her desire to help is no surprise to Mom. She describes Beth as empathetic; "she really goes out for the underdog."

Beth says that the events of September 11 make her very sad. "Well, it makes me sad that people would crash planes into the World Trade Center and the Pentagon." Beth's sadness turned to fear "after President Bush declared war." Her fear, however, was overshadowed by her belief that "America is strong and they [the soldiers] will help us a lot and it will help us win the war." She is very emotional as she describes the victims of the plane that crashed in Pennsylvania. She believed that "they were gonna go for the White House, so they crashed the plane in Pennsylvania so the White House would be saved. I thought they [the victims] were very brave." When she thinks about her own safety, Beth believes that, for the most part, she is safe. However, "whenever I hear a plane come over I'm kinda scared because people might be dropping bombs and stuff. I really don't know what happened and so that's why I'm kinda scared. So when I fall asleep, I always say a prayer that there won't be any bombs that go into my street or anywhere in New York." Beth empathizes with the children of Afghanistan and articulates her position clearly and with conviction.

> I feel bad for them because they're poor and have to face war right now. I feel good and happy for them because we're dropping food from planes. I also feel bad because the Taliban is taking their food. And I hate the Taliban because they are the ones that crashed the planes in the World Trade Center and the Pentagon, and I don't like them because they're stealing all the food

from the kids and their clothes and stuff and money. They barely even have enough money for food. Yeah, and they are burning down houses and sending anthrax in the mail.

In her spare time Beth likes to read, although she is very particular about what she reads. "I like to read, not like hard books because they are sometimes complicated and the words are big and I can't read them." Beth likes to read scary stories "'cause I like reading scary things." Beth's love for animals comes through again when she talks about the book *Dear Mr. Henshaw.* Her favorite character in the book is the dog, Bandit, "'cause I like dogs and he would never get mad at his owner even when all his owner would do is drive around." *Stuart Little,* another favorite, excites Beth. Stuart, however, is not her favorite character. That position goes to the cat in the story "who is always dropping Stuart. He wouldn't keep him in his mouth and he didn't obey. I like that because sometimes my cat doesn't obey when I tell her to do things."

As with most 11-year-olds, Beth also watches some TV in her spare time, even though "I don't have cable anymore." She makes a very serious face and says that it is Ann's fault because of MTV. Her mom didn't want Ann or anyone else in the family to watch MTV, so she removed cable television from the home. "So all I get to watch are baseball games, which is for boys, and Mary's little baby shows." This doesn't deter her from watching what other kids her age might be watching on TV. She loves to visit her friends who do have cable, and she watches a show called *SpongeBob SquarePants.* Beth laughs as she describes the characters in this cartoon. These include SpongeBob, Patrick (the starfish), and Squidward, who works at the Crusty Crab restaurant. She isn't too crazy about Squidward, whom she describes as "not nice and a mean neighbor." "Squidward is mean and makes fun of SpongeBob," and he "feels sad and grows really small."

Rugrats is another show Beth tries to catch when she is visiting her friends. She describes a character in the show, Angelica, whom she doesn't like and feels is "very mean." "She is always telling lies and makes everyone feel bad and she is always being a brat." The character Tommy is her favorite because "he is brave and he comforts his friends." She also likes Tommy because he is "actionful." He likes to investigate and "find stuff out," which is obviously something that Beth really enjoys. Another character in the show is Chuckie and Beth describes him as "boring." When asked to explain this, Beth says Chuckie "is always afraid of things, like he's afraid of the man on the oatmeal box."

Having friends is important to Beth. "I only have one friend and her name is Susan." She explains that she has more friends but Susan is "my best, best friend." Beth says that Susan is "fun" and "she likes a lot of things I like." Susan does not attend Beth's school, but they spend a lot of time together outside of school since Susan lives nearby. Even though they are good friends now, Beth says she started out several years ago being friends with Dan, Susan's brother. Beth remembers clearly that at first Susan was always being mean to her. However, after awhile she began to think that Dan had become "just so dumb, so I liked Susan and now she is my friend." They clearly have a lot in common. They are in the same grade and like to play outside, listen to music, and have sleepovers. At these sleepovers they have long "girl" talks. Sometimes these talks include Beth telling Susan about how her feelings get hurt at school. Beth describes Susan saying, "I wish I could help you, and she'd help me and then I'd help her with things that happen to her."

Beth's school, with approximately 250 students, is located right on a busy street in an urban community and serves an ethnically diverse population. Half the school's students are African American, with a smaller percentage (less than 10%) coming from Hispanic and Native American or Pacific Islander groups. Close to 60% of the students in Beth's school are eligible for free or reduced-price lunch. When talking about her school, Beth focuses on the fact that it is a public school and "we just got a new playground." She says all the kids want to play on the new playground but they have to take turns with the younger children in the school. She complains that 15 minutes is just not long enough for recess. Her classroom is in a trailer that is attached to the school. "My classroom has bookshelves, computers, file cabinets, coat hangers, and a clock." She also says that there is a rug in the room for sitting, but she usually does not get to use it. The desks are organized into rows, and she describes her teacher as "just usually giving us work." She does enjoy when her teacher gives them mystery puzzles and then "we have to figure out what the thing is." Academically, Beth's school has generally performed slightly below similar schools in the areas of English language arts and mathematics, and comparably in science. In the past year, the school met its state's standards for mathematics performance but did not meet standards set for English language arts.

As for her classmates, Beth expresses some frustration about trying to make friends with one girl at school. Beth says that this particular girl makes fun of her. She explains that, "I like her, but she doesn't like me." When pushed to come up with reasons why this girl doesn't like her, Beth attributes it to race. "I'm white and she's black, so she really doesn't like white people." Beth indicates that while she talks to her mom a lot, she chose not to mention this problem to her. "I don't want her [the classmate] to get mad, so I don't tell my mom."

Beth's teacher, Ms. Connelly, can see these friendship difficulties in class. "She never really has made a best friend and is not part of the 'in' group." Ms. Connelly attributes this to the fact that the girls in her class have been together since kindergarten, and it is very difficult for someone new to become part of their group. Despite Beth's difficulties, Ms. Connelly says that Beth is well-adjusted to her class and "she likes me, is comfortable with me, and likes my class." Beth is in total agreement with her teacher. "My teacher is nice and smart." When asked how she knows her teacher is smart she says, "'Cause she wouldn't be a teacher if she wasn't smart. Plus she knows all the math things and stuff."

Mom concurs that friendships have not always come easily for Beth, but her relationships are "much improved this year." Mom attributes this to Beth's growing up a bit. Earlier, she was "kind of immature, basically saying what was on her mind." She remembers when Beth told her grandmother that her breath smelled. Mom uses this as an example of Beth saying things that are on her mind without thinking about how they might hurt others. However, Mom believes that Beth is becoming more sensitive, although she still worries about the "social part" of development. Mom has worked with Beth to get her to understand that while it is important to tell the truth, there are times when it might be better to say nothing. Mom tells her, "If it's not something that builds someone up, then don't say it."

"Building someone up" is something that Mom does quite a bit with Beth. She is concerned about Beth's lack of self-confidence. At Beth's former parochial school, if you were not "the smartest or the prettiest or the most popular, you didn't fit in." Mom believes that Beth's not fitting that mold has contributed to her lack of confidence. Beth's lack of self-confidence is something Mom has communicated to Beth's teachers because she knows that self-confidence is so closely related to achievement. Mom reports "she struggles in just about every area of academics, but she perseveres, never giving up." Mom worries particularly about the fact that academics have come so easily to her other children, which Beth has clearly noticed. "There's Beth, always struggling, plugging along, and very aware of that."

Mom and Ms. Connelly concur that Beth sometimes has difficulty with reading. According to Mom, Beth also has some difficulties in math, science, and social studies. Ms. Connelly believes that part of her weakness in math is in the problem-solving area, which she says is clearly related to her reading problems.

As Beth describes her experiences reading in school, she is keenly aware of her difficulties. "We read in groups and I don't usually read because I can't read good and sometimes when I read, the words get blurry. I don't feel like reading because it's hard for me."

Beth also identifies math as a subject she doesn't like "because it's a little hard for me, and sometimes I don't get it." Beth is grateful for the help she gets from her teacher. "My teacher helps me 'cause I'm not very smart in math so she [Ms. Connelly] likes to come over to my desk and help me." Beth says that when the teacher helps her, she seems to do better.

There are some things about school that Beth enjoys. Her favorite subjects are spelling, speech, recess, and gym. When describing her gym teacher, Beth says, "I like him because he is so nice and we get to play mad ball, pinball, football, soccer, and even hockey."

She says that her class "doesn't have any bad kids in it." Beth believes that all of the bad kids are in the other sixth grade (there are two classes at every grade level), and she is glad not to be in that classroom. If students do misbehave in her class, the teacher just says "shh" and then "erases one of the five respect points on the board."

Mom agrees that the class has a good mix of children. The class is "even tempered and pretty small, around 18." However, when describing this urban public school, Mom says, "There are a lot of tough customers. I'll say there's a lot of kids for whom violence is their M.O." She expresses some concern about the fighting that takes place among both boys and girls. Beth isn't really troubled or even frightened by the fighting, according to Mom. "She just thinks it's ridiculous."

Recently, Beth received a progress report from school. Mom's reaction to the report is that it's "not so hot." In the report, Beth's teacher indicated her lack of focus and lack of attention. Mom said that when Beth read the report, she disagreed and was "indignant" over it. Mom called the teacher and has a conference scheduled for later in the week.

The family is currently trying to decide where to send Beth for middle school. Her elementary school only goes to grade six and feeds into the city's two middle schools. The concern over the middle school is its size, its poor academic record, and its tough population. Mom feels that Beth would just get lost in such a school. She is afraid that Beth will fall through the cracks and will not get her needs met in such an environment. The family is considering private school or a move into the suburbs.

Despite some school and social difficulties, Beth is "outgoing and empathetic," says Mom. When it comes to looking forward to her future, Beth is hoping to be a teacher or a veterinarian. "I like teachers and it looks fun, and I also would want to be a veterinarian because I love animals." This comes as no surprise when you think about the activities she likes to do.

DISCUSSION QUESTIONS

1. Characterize Beth's overall self-concept. In what domains has Beth likely developed a negative self-concept? A positive one? Discuss how you think the various domains of self-concept have contributed to her overall self-concept and speculate on what factors might affect her self-concept over time.

2. Based on what you know about Beth from the case, at what stage of Kohlberg's moral reasoning might Beth be? Justify your answer with evidence from the case.

3. What effect might Beth's lack of peer relationships in school have on her as she moves into adolescence? To what do you attribute her lack of friends? What effect might her friendship with Susan have as she moves into adolescence? Support your ideas with evidence from your course and the case.

4. What actions might Beth's teacher take to improve Beth's academic self-concept? How would Beth's own efficacy in this area affect her self-esteem?

5. Using information from your course and from the case, theorize as to what effect others' expectations might be having on Beth's achievement in school and in social situations. Cite evidence for your theories. Critique your own theories.

6. How might Ms. Connelly deal with the apparent racial tension that exists between Beth and the African American student? How could she use the research on culturally relevant pedagogy to create an environment where all students feel welcome?

7. Who are Beth's role models? What qualities of both real people and media characters does Beth seem to admire? How do you think this has affected her socialization?

APPLYING THEORETICAL PERSPECTIVES

1. Which of the cognitive theories you have studied thus far can be best used to explain Beth's cognitive development, and in particular, her cognitive difficulties? Defend your answer using information from the case and from your text.

2. According to Erikson, what developmental challenge or crisis does Beth currently face? Based on the case, analyze the potential risks Beth faces in overcoming this challenge, and suggest ways that Beth's teacher and family might assist Beth to meet this challenge. Support your suggestions by showing how they are consistent with Erikson's theory.

3. What might Piaget say about the apparent learning environment in Beth's current classroom? What might Vygotsky say? What methods might Vygotsky suggest for improving Beth's academic performance?

Also see "Connecting Across Cases" questions 4 and 9, in the Introduction to this book.

CLASS ACTIVITY

1. Create a role play in which Beth is not included in an activity where her classmates are forming groups along their previous friendship patterns. What strategies might Ms. Connelly use to address this problem?

RESEARCH SUGGESTION

1. What are signs of a learning disability that Beth's mother or teacher might observe? What would be appropriate actions for her mother or

teacher to take to determine if she has a disability? How might having a learning disability relate to a child's social problems?

READINGS AND RESOURCES

LD OnLine at www.ldonline.org

LD OnLine is a service of The Learning Project at WETA, Washington, DC, in association with The Coordinated Campaign for Learning Disabilities. It provides extensive information and resources for parents, youth, and teachers.

National Center for Learning Disabilities at www.ncld.org

This Web site provides information and resources for parents and teachers on living and working with students with learning disabilities.

Chapman, J. W. (1989). Learning disabled children's self-concepts. *Review of Educational Research, 58,* 347–371.

This study investigates the impact of learning disabilities on children's view of their competence, social acceptance, and self-worth.

Kavale, K. A., & Forness, S. R. (1996). Social skill deficits and learning disabilities: A meta-analysis. *Journal of Learning Disabilities, 29*(3), 226–237. (Summary of key sections available at www.coe.unt.edu/wood/images/edsp_57208888.htm)

This article is a meta-analysis of studies that have investigated the relationships between social skills and learning disabilities.

SEVEN

EDWARD

Full of Life and Always Moving

———————◄•◆•►———————

PRIMARY AND SECONDARY ISSUES

Primary Issues:	Secondary Issues:
• Attention deficit hyperactivity disorder and the influence of context on youth with disabilities • Social and emotional development and out-of-school activities • Mentoring, adult-youth relationships, mediated learning	• Social cognition and social skills • Multicultural friendships • Peer relationships

CASE

"Oh, no!" cries Edward as he crouches on the stage, staring out at the audience in mock horror with his big brown eyes wide open. His shoulders slump and his face is crestfallen as he stands up and groans, "We're never going to get to Florida."

His friends giggle and most of the 30 parents watching the final performances by their children in this storytelling camp smile as he spins an extravagant tale of the burning bridges and colliding cars that filled his family's last vacation. Edward's mother puts her face in her hands as she listens to her often unpredictable son navigate from one catastrophe to another. At her side, Edward's stepfather and grandmother also seem surprised at this imaginative account of their family history.

His mother had seen the camp as a way for Edward to improve his reading skills and learn to become more responsible for himself. The camp was based at a local college where Edward receives specialized help in reading. His mother and stepfather knew the literacy clinic supervisor, Robin, a professor at the college who was also the head teacher for the storytelling portion of the camp. The two-week camp was offered free of charge to any fifth or sixth grade child in the city who had received tutoring or clinic services from the college's many community-based programs. The campers stayed overnight for the whole two weeks in small student residential houses and college dorms staffed by college student counselors. The children came from diverse ethnic backgrounds, although a majority, like Edward, are from African American families. Additionally, most of the children attended inner city public schools, several were from religious inner city schools, and a few were from suburban schools. For many of these youth who struggle with academic problems, it was their first experience of living in a college community and the first time away from their families.

Edward is a 12-year-old African American boy who lives with his mother, stepfather, grandmother, and six-year-old sister in a quiet residential neighborhood in a mid-sized northeastern city. Edward's special education teacher at the science and technology magnet school that he attends indicated that he could benefit from help over the summer. As a fifth grader, he was reading at a 1.9 grade level. Edward said that one of his reasons for coming to camp was "because I need a lot of extra help on my reading. I sometimes don't understand what I am reading because I am trying to read really fast. . . . My mom says that I need a lot of extra help. That's why I needed to go there."

Although he liked the literacy clinic programs and wanted to do better at reading, Edward had been reluctant to come to camp at first. His mother called Robin several times with information that she thought she needed to know about Edward. Robin said that his mother was very "caring and protective" and that the family provided a strong support network for him. His mother made careful arrangements for Edward to receive his medications for attention deficit hyperactivity and a tic disorder and cautioned Robin that Edward wasn't sure he wanted to attend the camp. Edward's stepfather is a lawyer at another university where Robin's husband teaches. Robin said that his stepfather had a reputation for speaking his mind even if others did not want to hear what he said. When she first heard that Edward had signed up for the storytelling camp, she said, "I thought, 'Oh, wow! We're getting Edward. We've got to gear up for this one.' . . . We anticipated some problems, but those were never realized. . . . He was fine."

On the first night, Edward's parents dropped him off and his mother said, "See you in two weeks." Robin says she thought, "This boy might need some tender loving care. . . . So I went over to his dorm with him and settled him in and helped him make his bed." However, she says that he seemed to fit right in and was very socially adept, making friends right from the start. Edward says that he hoped camp would allow him to "have some time to myself" and "to spend time with new people." He quickly established friendships with several boys in his dorm and with their counselors, Nick and Mike, who talked with them and set up funny evening activities. One night Nick and Mike created a haunted house, putting a tape player of spooky noises under their bed as a way of promoting group bonding through a shared scary experience. In contrast to his usual bravado, Edward was very scared, a feeling he shared with his roommates who quickly became his close friends. Mike says that Edward missed his family and had a hard time adjusting to being away from home for the first time, especially at the beginning of camp when he wanted to call home constantly. Even later in the camp he called home every night, sometimes twice a night, just to talk. Edward says that he feels very close to his mother "'cause she is loving and 'cause she cares about me and I care about her." She often helps him with his school projects, and although Edward has chores that he has to complete daily, his mother "sometimes does the dishes for me."

Despite his reluctance to come to camp and his longing for his family, Edward seemed a perfect fit with the storytelling activities. Robin says that one of his greatest strengths was his "ability to take the stage. He is not self-conscious in front of an audience. He is willing to do some things that make him look a little foolish, which is exactly what you need to do as a storyteller." On the first day, she asked the storytelling campers to write down some of the stories in their lives using open-ended questions as prompts. Then she asked who would share a family story. Without a trace of embarrassment, Edward immediately jumped up and read, "When I was born, I was huge! I weighed 13 pounds." Physically Edward was still bigger than many of the other campers, but his willingness to laugh at himself made him approachable.

On another day, the storytelling campers went to a vintage shop to pick out clothes and props for their stories. Many children were at first hesitant to try on the strange clothes. But Edward and his friend Matt pulled on some long dresses and danced about the store. Edward says that dancing is a big part of who he is. "I dance everywhere. I break-dance." His willingness to take risks and be silly helped to loosen up the other youth. Soon everyone was trying on clothes and hats and laughing. Robin says, "It was a great day for the camp." And later in the day the other campers were still saying, "Oh, did you see Edward dress up in that dress?"

While Edward excelled at oral storytelling, he had difficulty with activities that required reading and writing. Diagnostic reading tests conducted at the clinic showed that he could read fluently but had very poor comprehension of what he read. With a little coaxing, however, Edward was willing to try all of the camp activities, most of which used literacy skills across multiple modalities. One project involved selecting and reading a storybook that he then had to read and act out for a younger child at a nearby elementary school. Edward practiced and practiced, refining his pacing, working on good eye contact, and creating voices for the characters in his chosen book.

Robin said that one of the most involved projects was "to tell a story from your own experience and develop it to make other people enjoy it . . . to really relive it for the audience." They began work on the stories during the first week of camp and continued until the last day. The stories were to be performed at the camp closing, and storytellers were required to establish a timeline for their life, include some dramatic episodes, and write and rewrite their story. Edward was the only student who wrote a story that Robin and her co-teacher, Beth, knew from the start was not true. She and Beth talked about whether they should confront and discourage Edward, but decided instead to let him work on it. Edward "went through the different stages that he had to in working on it, and thinking about it, and adding to it, and practicing it."

Then the day before the final performance he came to Robin and said, "You know my story is not true." Robin replied, "Yeah, I've known for a long time, but you were so into it, and you wanted it to be true, and you tried to convince people that it was true. So that tells you something about storytelling too!" Edward performed his tall tale with relish at the closing.

Robin viewed Edward's admission that his story was untrue as a "growth experience for him. I think that it took some gumption on his part to decide that that was important. And I think that took some trust." She feels that her connection to Edward is what helped to avoid the problems they had been led to expect. The connection between Edward and Robin was evident even in the follow-up meetings held once a month during the school year following the camp. Edward was working on an Internet assignment and about halfway through the project his attention was wandering. Noticing that he had just cut his curly hair short, Robin walked over and said, "Edward, would you allow me to do one thing I really would like to do?" Glancing cautiously at her, he said, "What's that?" She replied, "Can I rub your head?" Surprised but apparently pleased, he said, "Okay, you can rub my head," and afterward he returned to his assignment with renewed focus.

Edward repeatedly tested the boundaries of his counselors and teachers in small mischievous ways, by back talking, teasing other campers, incessant talking, and wandering off task. He later complained that at camp "you have to do work every five seconds!" Robin said, "He will test you to see what he can get away with. But then, when you call him on it, he's okay." One day during a snack, Edward and his friends were exchanging notes with phone numbers. They started tossing wads of paper at each other and then began throwing the papers into each others' drinks and laughing. When Edward started pulling the wet papers out and scattering them around the table, Robin said, "That's enough, Edward. As a matter of fact, you are going to throw those papers away. You are going to clean the table for me." Edward started to reply, "Oh, I couldn't," but Robin cut him off. "No, Edward, you're going to do me the favor of cleaning up the papers and clearing the table for me." Glancing at his friends, Edward tried to humor his way out, "Well, why don't you do me a favor and pay all my bills?" Straight-faced, Robin replied, "No way! I can't even pay all my own bills." As the group laughed, Robin continued, "No, Edward, right now you are going to do the favor for me." With a sheepish grin, Edward did clean up the entire table.

One of the camp goals was to promote multicultural friendships among its diverse group of children. Since the children came from many different schools, few of them knew each other before the camp. The storytelling group included four boys and eight girls. The boys were two Caucasian youth, Matt and Kyle, and two African American youth, Edward and Darrell. All of the girls except one were African American. The boys seemed to click immediately and Edward was very "tight" with Matt throughout the camp. The children lived together in the college's small residential houses separated by sex. They also ate all meals together and the camp curriculum included many team-building activities to promote friendship. Initially the sole Caucasian girl was off by herself while the rest of the girls giggled and played. However, halfway through the camp, she asked one of the other girls to braid her hair in cornrows, and subsequently she joined in most activities with the other girls.

Edward had many friends among both the boys and the girls and was one of the most popular campers. On occasion, Robin said Edward seemed to need to "talk big" to compensate for his self-consciousness about his academic problems. The camp included children with a wide range of abilities, and some youth had learning problems more severe than Edward's. Kyle, a small boy who needed extensive help with all of the projects, was the target of much teasing, and Robin admits that she had to intervene to prevent Edward from "bullying him." Edward was not a "goody goody" she says, although most of the time his willingness to take risks and try new things spurred the group's imagination. And the collaborative nature of most camp activities helped to encourage peer support.

Edward says that the best part of camp was "getting some girls' phone numbers." He had several girlfriends during the camp and unlike many boys his age, he enjoyed talking with them and often sat with them on the buses during field trips. At times he did not know how to express his interest and teased the girls about how they looked or something they said. He embarrassed one girl, Tanya, so often that after one field trip on which he was particularly mean to Tanya, Robin pulled him aside and said, "How do you think your behavior is making Tanya feel?" Edward shrugged, and Robin said, "Well it makes her feel bad. So what can you do about that?" Edward later talked to Tanya and apologized for his taunting. On the last day of camp, he announced that he was "getting married" to his newest girlfriend!

Mike, one of the storytelling counselors, says that Edward was most out of control at the end of his medication cycles later in the afternoon. When the medication was wearing off, Edward would become "very silly and very funny, just trying to be a funny guy. And he had a hard time controlling his body and controlling his actions and his choices." The most extreme instance occurred after a field trip where Edward was overdue for his medications because he had forgotten to take them with him. He started jumping and running and dancing through the flower beds on the street. Mike says it seemed like he "just couldn't control what he was doing. He didn't really understand the actions. It was like he was crawling out of his skin sometimes. We had to hold him because he was just jumping and running around." Mike, who is a special education teacher, said that he often uses touch as a "sensory push" to help children regain control. He kept a careful watch on Edward's medication schedule and made sure that he never missed a dose, although Edward took the medication himself and was usually not difficult to manage. Mike describes Edward as "energetic, happy, fun, likeable, and a good kid who really did try to work hard and do his best. Full of life and always moving."

Robin admits that Edward could be difficult to manage in a regular school classroom. Edward complains that schools have too many rules and especially objects to not being able to get up without permission. He finds subjects like social studies and math difficult and says that his teacher does not always provide the help he needs. "When we ask her an important question, she just says put your hand down now. Then I say, 'But I have to ask you a question 'cause you are the teacher. You are supposed to answer kids' questions.'" Sometimes when he persistently asks her if he can get a drink, "she ignores me and I just keep on saying it and she still ignores me." However, Edward says, "I've never been to the principal. I'm a good boy."

He has many interests outside of school such as Harry Potter books, BET (Black Entertainment Television), rap and jazz music, cooking spaghetti and baked macaroni, and sports. He emphasizes that sports have taught him "good sportsmanship. It's like you're playing and . . . you get out like [in] baseball. You go to a base and they get you out. Some people just cop an attitude and that's not good sportsmanship. If you don't cop an attitude, then you have good sportsmanship. Don't get all angry about it. It's only a game."

Robin agrees that Edward is a "good kid" and says that she is grateful to have had him in her storytelling group. "He was a pleasure . . . . I'm glad that he was with us . . . . He was important to the group. He was one of the kids who let it all hang out, and that helped other kids relax."

Edward came to all but two follow-up sessions. Of the 24 children attending the camp, only 12 consistently attended the follow-up sessions. His attendance and participation, however, were interrupted by his tutoring appointments, which occurred during the same time period as the follow-up sessions. He is now receiving tutoring at the college for mathematics as well as reading. This summer he has signed up for a math, science, and technology group at the camp that includes activities in space exploration. He is also working on a science fair project for school about airplanes and will be visiting a space camp in Montreal with his class. He was disappointed to learn that the camp was earthbound. "I thought we were really going to go into space." He says that he is not sure he wants to go to the college-based camp again this summer, but his mother wants him to go. Only time will tell if his space camp teachers can launch this reluctant cadet on his next adventure in learning.

DISCUSSION QUESTIONS

1. What signs of attention deficit hyperactivity disorder (ADHD) are apparent in Edward's behavior? How do the teachers and counselors manage his behavior and encourage the development of social cognitive abilities?

2. How did Robin's relationship with Edward facilitate his learning and development? What specifically did she do to help him build skills and learn to control his own behavior? Discuss her relationship with him within the larger context of research on how adult/child relationships outside the family facilitate development.

3. Edward is described as one of the most popular children in the camp. What do you think accounts for his ability to easily make friends? How did the camp activities and teachers promote formation of friendships even across racial and ethnic groups?

4. Despite his history of difficulties in school, Edward was very successful at this camp. What are some differences between school settings and after school programs that might account for this success? How do after school settings like this camp promote social and cognitive development in children?

APPLYING THEORETICAL PERSPECTIVES

1. At 12 years old, Edward is likely resolving Erikson's Industry vs. Inferiority (Stage 4) and moving into Identity vs. Role Confusion (Stage 5).
   a. How do you think Erikson would characterize Edward's resolution of Stage 4? Use specific examples from the case (especially school and camp) to explain your answer.

    b. As Edward moves into Stage 5, what issues and experiences in his life will influence his resolution of this stage?

    c. Erikson uses the term "community of life cycles" to characterize the influence we all have on each other. What do you think Edward needs from those around him in order to successfully resolve Stage 5?

2. What might Howard Gardner say about the types of intelligence fostered by the storytelling camp? Give specific examples of how different types of intelligence might be fostered through storytelling.

CLASS ACTIVITIES

1. Create a role play to show how you might respond if Edward were making fun of another camper's story.

2. Considering Edward's strengths and weaknesses, how should the space camp teacher prepare for his inclusion in the camp? Design and present an activity that you think would engage Edward and help build skills in mathematics, science, and technology.

RESEARCH SUGGESTION

1. Conduct research on the frequency of attention deficit hyperactivity disorder diagnoses in youth in the United States today. In class, debate whether this disorder is overdiagnosed or not. What types of treatments are used with youth with this disability and what factors influence the type of treatment used?

READINGS AND RESOURCES

National Institute of Mental Health. (2003). *Attention deficit hyperactivity disorder.* Available at www.nimh.nih.gov/publicat/adhd.cfm

This Web site provides extensive information on ADHD and other disabilities.

National Dissemination Center for Children with Disabilities. (2004). *Attention deficit/hyperactivity disorder.* Fact Sheet 19 (FS19). Available at www.nichcy.org/pubs/factshe/fs19txt.htm

This Center provides educational information and resources for advocacy for children with disabilities.

EIGHT

FRANK

Confronting Change and
Taking a Stand in Middle School

by Gina Ciccone

───◦•◦───

PRIMARY AND SECONDARY ISSUES

Primary Issues:	Secondary Issues:
• Depression	• Empathy, prosocial behaviors
• Identity development	• Ecological theory
• Peer groups/peer pressure/	• Motivation strategies
cliques/social isolation	
• Moral development	

CASE

Thirteen-year-old Frank lives in rural upstate New York with Mom, Dad, and his 15-year-old sister, Karen. The family lives in a large farmhouse that sits on a hill off a county highway. The house is surrounded by woods, and there are no other houses in sight. Next to the house there is a large barn that currently houses the family's geese, chickens, and guinea hens. Nearby is an orchard of apple and peach trees.

Frank has another sister, Jess, who is Mom's daughter from a previous marriage. Jess lives in Vermont with her husband and two-year-old son, Jack. Three years ago, Frank and his family moved from the suburbs of a midwestern city to their present home to be closer to Jess and Frank's elderly grandmother, who lives in a nursing home.

Frank is a tall boy with a slightly disheveled appearance—baggy clothes and thick reddish-brown hair. He sports a warm, amiable smile, and he's friendly but not overly talkative. When you talk to him, you get a clear impression of both youthful innocence and shrewd perceptiveness.

Frank is the youngest child in a well-educated family. Mom, Dad, and Jess all hold doctorate degrees. Mom is a scientist for a government agency, and Dad is a college professor. Mom describes Jess as "a very earnest, hardworking, ambitious, smart young woman." Frank's sister Karen is at the top of her tenth-grade class and is applying for early college admission. Mom describes her as "driven, funny, smart, quick [and] very hardworking." When asked to describe Frank, Mom laughs and says,

> At this current age right now, a mystery to me. He is a mystery to me. As a mother of a son, I don't understand him. . . . He's a whole different personality than my other children. . . . He won't tell me anything. He doesn't talk. He doesn't share anything.

She goes on to say that Frank is "smart, funny, [and] a caring guy" who is also "extraordinarily stubborn." She cites empathy as one of his strongest traits and says he's very caring with little Jack and the various animals he tends.

According to Mom, Frank is also extremely kind and loving toward his grandmother and other elderly people. Frank regularly brings his dog, Tiger, to his grandmother's nursing home so the residents can interact with a pet. During a recent visit to the home, Frank noticed an elderly woman sitting nearby who was muttering and gesturing toward her mouth. Frank sat down next to her and watched her and talked to her for a while. Later, he told Mom that the woman thought she was picking blueberries. Mom believes Frank's kindness is something that "set[s] him apart from some of the other kids" his age.

As evidence of Frank's stubbornness, Mom points to his bedroom, which she repeatedly tries to get him to straighten up. Frank admits "it's a pretty messy room." In addition to the usual furnishings, Frank has posters and clippings on the walls. One is an anti-smoking sign. Frank doesn't express many strong opinions, but he'll ardently tell you, "I *hate* smoking." Also on the walls are video game posters, a *Mad Magazine* cover that pokes fun at rapper Eminem, and a *Pinocchio* picture. *Pinocchio* is Frank's favorite cartoon movie. Mom says she's tired of dealing with Frank's mess but doesn't quite know how to solve the problem. "If I do go in there and pick something up, he gets irritated."

As further proof of Frank's stubbornness, Mom points to how hard it sometimes is to get him to give up favorite clothes so she can wash them. "He wore the same pair of pajama bottoms for five days. He even wore them under his pants." Mom laughs as she reports,

> I tease him, too, about his clothes—his low-hanging pants. What happens is, if he's bending over for something and his boxers are hanging out, I might pinch them, and I tell him, "Frank, I actually like it when you wear your pants that way because I can tell when you've changed your boxers."

She ruefully adds, "I'm probably not as kind as I should be." But this gentle teasing from Mom doesn't seem to bother Frank, who describes himself as having "a good sense of humor."

Frank's favorite music group is Sum 41, a pop-punk band, but he's not sure why. "It's just one of those things." He also likes to listen to classical music when he reads, which is one of his favorite pastimes. He prefers the fantasy genre, and he's quick to name Robert Jordan as his favorite author. Jordan writes series of epic fantasy novels; individual books range from 700 to over 1,000 pages. Frank is a voracious reader. On average, he reads two of Jordan's books a month. The one he's currently reading is over 1,000 pages long. Although Frank likes reading fantasy, he's not a fan of the Harry Potter books. "I didn't think they were that good."

Playing video games is also one of Frank's favorite pastimes. He particularly likes *Age of Empires,* which is an epic strategy game that challenges the player to build and conquer ancient civilizations. Frank usually plays it after school "for about an hour." He has a computer, but he doesn't use the Internet. This is his choice, not his parents'. When asked why, Frank simply states, "I just don't like it." He also watches television, but he doesn't have a favorite show. "I just generally watch what's on," which sometimes includes the news.

In addition to reading and playing video games, Frank participates in a number of other activities. He plays soccer on a community team and he's in a ski club at school. He's also a Boy Scout and a member of a 4-H Club. Frank's reasons for joining the Boy Scouts and 4-H Club have little to do with the underlying philosophies of the groups. "It's just more fun than, you know, after school, than [to] just sit home and watch TV and do nothing." He likes the physical aspects of the activities and being with other kids. Mom describes a recent hike Frank went on with his Boy Scout troop: "They went to some rock that's shaped like a rabbit or something [and] he came back and he said, 'Mom, it really does look like a rabbit!' And he was really impressed. I don't think that many thirteen-year-old boys would be impressed."

Frank also spends a lot of time working with animals. Once a week he volunteers at a farm that takes in horses that have been abused, abandoned, or "put out to pasture." Frank makes sure the horses have enough water and he mucks out their stalls. As part of his 4-H Club activities, he also drives a team of oxen at a local historic farm, which is something he really enjoys. At home, Frank is responsible for taking care of his dog and the family's geese. It's his job to make sure the animals are fed, watered, and sheltered at night. When talking about the animals, he admits, "I haven't always been on top of taking care of them, but nothing bad has ever happened."

Mom agrees that Frank hasn't always been consistent about doing his chores at home. "He does those things in phases. We'll have a talking-to with him and say, 'Frank, this just isn't like you.' And then he'll do it without asking, and then other times, it's like, 'Frank, the geese's water was frozen—you need to take care of it.'"

In the past, Frank has also taken music lessons, but he quickly abandoned them because he "didn't want to practice." Mom describes Frank's experience with the lessons:

> We try stuff and then we have to fight with him to do it, so I just gave up. When we moved here I said, "Frank, what would you like to do?" And he said, "Well, I'd like to learn how to play the drums." So I said, "Okay, when we move to New York, we'll find a drum teacher." And we found someone down here, but he just didn't want to practice, so it was not a positive thing.
>
> Then, the next year, he really wanted to play trumpet in the band. We got this shiny trumpet, and he'd go outside with the trumpet, and that just lasted for about a week. And I feel like it was the practice and the teacher—and so, he didn't do that. And I think now he's afraid to try anything because it sets him up for—for failure, at least in the music department.

She adds, "He wants to do things perfectly right away."

Frank's family leads a busy life. When Mom and Dad aren't working, they're often driving Frank and Karen to their different activities. Before the family moved to New York, they frequently engaged in outdoor activities like camping, backpacking, and hiking. They haven't spent much time doing those things since the move, due to Frank and Karen's activities and the family's home improvement efforts. "We watch movies a lot together," says Mom. They either rent videos or go to a small movie theater in a nearby village. Dad and Karen also practice Buddhism, and they attend a local center together twice a week. Mom indicates that Buddhism doesn't appeal to her and that Frank doesn't have "any interest in meditating, sitting still for twenty minutes at a time and just quietly reflecting."

Frank and Karen occasionally argue over "petty stuff," like whose turn it is to use the computer or wash the dishes. Despite these squabbles, Frank describes his relationship with Karen as "pretty good." He would definitely feel comfortable talking to her about things that he didn't want to talk to Mom or Dad about. Mom describes the relationship between Frank and Karen as a good one, and she says they both get along well with older sister Jess.

Despite his affinity with animals, Frank's rural life is something he wishes he could change. He would much rather live in the family's previous suburban neighborhood. "I'm not near any of my friends. I'm not near any nice people." In the old neighborhood, "I could, like, go next door and talk to the guy next door, or I could [go] down the street to my friends." When he lived in the suburbs, Frank had lots of friends that he could hang out with, and "the school was just down the street, too." Things are very different here.

Mom says that Frank has had a difficult time making friends since the family moved to New York. When Frank mentions different kids in conversation, Mom has offered to take them on outings. "But he doesn't really take my offer to do that. And I think he's expressed that there's really no one at school that he feels quite like. I think in some sense he feels alone." Mom also observes, "I think that sometimes he's happy and sometimes he seems sad—he just seems sad. And that worries me—worries my husband and myself." Mom and Dad have talked about whether Frank might be depressed. Mom gets particularly worried about this when he shirks his chores and goes to his room to play video games, or "doesn't want to do things—doesn't feel motivated—just feels tired or wants to watch the TV."

"I don't really have a best friend," Frank says. His friends consist of a small group of kids at school. Frank attends seventh grade at a public middle school in a rural district. In school, he. primarily "hang[s] out" with three guys—Joey, Michael, and Tim—but they don't really talk outside of school. Joey is in Frank's Boy Scout troop, but they generally don't do any other activities together.

Frank also has some female friends at school, but he's quick to clarify that they're not "girlfriends." He says that he and his friends talk about "anything that pops up," like school, teachers, family, movies, and music. But his friends don't share his interest in reading. "No one reads much." There are things that Frank and his friends talk about that he wouldn't discuss with his parents, but, with a laugh, he declines to elaborate on what they are.

Frank describes his middle school as very "cliquish." He indicates that there is already a distinct "druggie" group. He's not sure which drugs are being used, but says that alcohol, tobacco, and marijuana are definitely in use. Last year, Frank caught one of his friends smoking, and he was so angry that he ignored the friend for a few days. They never talked about the incident, though.

Frank says his middle school also has cliques of "preppies," who are mostly the school athletes. It has a distinct group of "poor people," who are the economically disadvantaged kids. Cliques of "hood-rats" are the trouble makers of the school, and there's also a "punkish-type" clique. Finally, there's an "I don't care group," which is Frank's name for the kids who don't care about belonging to cliques. This is where he places himself.

Frank's science teacher, Mr. Groban, confirms that he doesn't belong to a clique.

> In general, Frank strikes me as a—I don't want to say a loner—but you can tell he's not going to go along with peer pressure too much. He tends to stick to himself. What I've noticed is that he really seems to enjoy talking to adults more than other kids—which is okay, I'm just saying that's what I've noticed. . . . He doesn't appear to have a large group of friends.

Mr. Groban, who is familiar with Frank's various activities, observes that "he appears to be into his own little—he goes by his own little thing and he probably will stay that way." Mr. Groban describes Frank as a "quiet" student, but adds that he "seems to have come out of his shell a little bit" after attending a recent school dance. "He seems to be more involved with people in the hallway. He doesn't seem to be such a loner."

Like Mom, Mr. Groban cites Frank's kindness as one of his strengths. "I think he's very kind hearted. I don't see a mean streak in him. I'm not saying he hasn't had a problem at all, I don't know. But he doesn't appear to be the type of kid that is going to be mean to other kids." Mr. Groban also says that Frank is "very knowledgeable about the world," and he counts this among Frank's strengths. "He's reading something, and he's listening to somebody, and he does have a good knowledge of world events."

Recently at school, Frank didn't want to stand for the Pledge of Allegiance as a way of protesting the war in Iraq. According to Mr. Groban, the teachers "weren't sure how to handle that because that's a touchy issue." Ultimately, Mr. Groban talked to Frank about it:

> And I just explained different things, you know, what legally you can do and what you can't do—whatever, I mean, it doesn't matter. And he was very receptive. I mean, no argument. Nobody was trying to scare him, I was just saying, just because you know where Baghdad is, most seventh graders don't. . . . So it's okay to have a political belief if you really know something, but just—I didn't want everyone following—whatever—because they don't really know. A lot of them are too young, or they just don't care. So, Frank was very receptive to our discussion. . . . [He] was very respectful. We actually had a good conversation, talking like two adults, and that was it.

And what does Frank think about school? "It's all just kind of the same. It's just school." When asked whether he likes his school, Frank responds, "No, not really." With a little hesitation, he goes on to say, "I feel—I feel like I'm losing my intelligence, slowly, since I moved here. Because I was at private school . . . I don't know." According to Mom, Frank's standardized test scores at his old school were in the high 90th percentile. Here, he's been scoring in the mid-70th to mid-80th percentiles. His grades are in the B to C range. Frank says he feels challenged enough by his schoolwork, but that he often finds school boring. He doesn't have a favorite subject. Occasionally lessons pique his interest, but "it depends on what I'm learning." He looks forward to going to school "on a day when it's time to get back a test that I think I did good on."

Frank candidly acknowledges that seventh grade has not been smooth. His biggest problem has been "handing in my homework." "Most of the time I do it, but I lose it or leave it at home." Frank's lack of organization is apparent during a recent class. He's attentive and he participates, but when it's time to take notes, he spends a few minutes rummaging around his books and pockets looking for a pen. When he realizes he doesn't have one, he doesn't ask a classmate for one but just listens to the teacher. After a couple of minutes, a classmate notices that Frank isn't writing. With a sigh, she hands him a pen, giving the impression that this happens frequently.

Language arts class is a particular problem for Frank. He hates the assignments, which largely consist of journal entries about designated topics. He asserts, with some vehemence, that "the journal entries are not—*ughh*—relevant to my life." Mom reports that "he turned in his journal, but he didn't write in it. He ripped the pages out so the teacher couldn't read the journal. All the pages were ripped out. So, it's been like that." She adds that Ms. Rowe, the language arts teacher, "talked to me for about an hour about this."

Frank is open about his dislike for Ms. Rowe, who is new to the middle school. He says, "I just don't get along with her" and "totally can't communicate with her." He also candidly admits that he does more goofing around in Ms. Rowe's class than in other classes, and that the time he spends on task in her class is about "fifty-fifty." Other than Ms. Rowe, Frank gets along with all of his teachers.

Mom describes Frank as "someone who doesn't care about schoolwork," which is problematic to Mom and Dad. In this family, it's also something that sets him apart. Frank has informed his parents that "I'm not going to get straight A's like Karen," and Mom thinks "having Karen as a sister has been a challenge for him." According to Mom, every school year "he starts out really excited, and then it's like a crash. He loses interest immediately." She describes Frank's current school situation midway through the school year:

> He's been having trouble. There's been more than one occasion, different things. In the early part of the year, we got a lot of calls from the guidance counselor and his teachers. I had to go in for a conference. It was the first time I had ever been called in for any of my kids.

"I was mortified," she adds, laughing. But for Mom and Dad, this is a serious issue. "I probably push too much on Frank. I want him to do good because I know he's smart. And I feel like seventh grade is when you really have to start studying now and doing homework because this counts," she explains.

Mom describes one phone call she received from the vice-principal, reporting Frank's misbehavior, and how she and Dad handled it:

> [Frank] had been caught by [Ms. Rowe], red-handed, marking up a lectern. Frank claimed it was an accident. So after that, my husband and myself had a very serious discussion with him. "This is not okay, this is not—." (Laughing). I'm like, "Frank, the next step is vandalism, and after vandalism, it's jail, and then what?" So we said, "if you get one more call—one more call—we're going to have to do something about ski club."

Mom reports that Frank made some adjustments after that; she hasn't received another call from school.

Mr. Groban, Frank's science teacher, has a simple explanation for Frank's school problems. "I think he's being lazy." But Mr. Groban doesn't see Frank as being different from many of his peers in this regard.

> Academically, I think he's very bright. I think he's not putting forth all the effort that he could, but then again, there are many boys not putting forth all the effort that they could (laughing). He's a good listener. When he wants to know something, he will listen. He doesn't have to study. He can just sit there, and he will listen, and he will get it. He will understand things.

Mr. Groban adds that Frank is "good at being self-directed if he's motivated." He works particularly well in activities that allow him to proceed on his own, rather than checking with the teacher after each step.

Mr. Groban believes that because Frank is "a naturally bright kid" who has "above average" academic ability, his parents and teachers get "on his case a little bit more" about schoolwork. He describes a recent talk he had with Frank:

> Two weeks ago, I took him aside and I said, "Frank, you have a week to straighten out the [language arts] grade and you have a week to start writing in your journal." And I didn't say it with, you know, self-esteem in mind. I didn't say it with, you know, "be a good boy and do it." I just said, "Do it." And I was kind of rough with him, but not threatening. And I just said, "Do it—you know you have the ability." And do you know, in a week he did everything. Now, I'm not saying it's going to stay that way.
>
> It's just the work habits. They can improve anytime he wants to. Whenever he wants to do something well, he can do it well. That's a good thing for him. He's lucky he has that ability. But, you know, we don't want him falling too far behind.

Mr. Groban says he'll continue to label Frank's work habits as "inconsistent until I see him really going for every subject, and we shouldn't have to remind him of things like that." He has talked with Frank's mom on several occasions and once with his dad, although he points out that middle school teachers at this school have limited time to meet with parents of their 130+ students. He believes that Frank's parents understand that it is up to Frank to change his habits.

While Frank's school situation has improved since the beginning of the school year, Mom believes that school is not a "positive experience" for Frank, and she remains frustrated by the school system. She believes Frank is "a challenge to reach," and she contends that "this school system is not reaching him. It's letting him down. It's just boring him to death and he's not trying." She is also frustrated by the limited time parents get with teachers at conferences. Mom and Dad have looked into sending Frank to one of the private schools in the area, but Frank has resisted, arguing that they're all "too preppy."

As for Frank's future, Mom says she just wants him to live to "his potential."

> I want him to like himself and love himself—and feel good about himself. And I want him to have options in life. I don't want him to be backed into a corner, and sometimes I'm afraid of that because of what I see. I can't help it. I'm his mother and that's what I bring to the relationship—he's going to have to deal with it (laughing)!

Mr. Groban speculates about Frank's future, too, and gives his perspective.

> I believe he's just at this age thing and he'll snap out of it. That's what we're all hoping for, and I really think he will. . . . I think he will have a very good high school career because I think in high school they're more on, you know, the testing. He'll do well on testing. And I think he'll do fine in college. But I think at this age he's not doing all of the little things we would like him to do.

As for Frank, he doesn't have any particular high school or college aspirations at this point. He thinks he might like to be a pilot someday, but he's not sure in what capacity, whether as a career or merely a hobby. "I just like flying." And although he likes working with animals, he doesn't envision a career with them. When asked whether he has any challenges to overcome in the future, Frank replies, "Nothing I can think of." But then he gives his amiable smile and earnestly adds, "—except I'm lazy."

DISCUSSION QUESTIONS

1. How has Frank exhibited empathetic and altruistic behaviors? What cognitive and emotional developmental milestones are required for such behaviors? Is Frank a typical teenager with regard to such behaviors? Why or why not? Support your answer with details from the case and information from your course.

2. Frank is experimenting with the identity of "nonconformist." Do you agree or disagree? Why?

3. Is Frank really lazy? What would motivational theorists have to say about Frank, especially the attributions he makes regarding his successes and failures?

4. What do Frank's parents and teachers see as the source of his motivational problems? What types of approaches have they tried with him? What else might they do to address Frank's current failure to live up to his potential?

5. In Mr. Groban's place, would you have handled the Pledge of Allegiance situation in the same manner or in a different manner? Defend your position using information from your course and what you know about Frank from the case.

6. With regard to the Pledge of Allegiance, Frank has disobeyed a rule because it is inconsistent with his personal belief about the war in Iraq. Based on other information from the case and what you know about Kohlberg's theory of moral development, at what level of moral reasoning is Frank operating? Support your position with details from the case and information from your course.

7. Do you agree with Frank's mother that Frank might be depressed? Why or why not? What does research on depression in adolescence suggest might be indicative of depression in Frank's case?

8. As a school counselor, what might you suggest to Frank's teachers as a means to engage Frank (or any student new to the school) in more social and peer activities? What does research suggest are the risks of social isolation? What are the benefits of involvement in peer relationships?

APPLYING THEORETICAL PERSPECTIVES

1. Bronfenbrenner might contend the changes observed in Frank are the consequences of changes in the "ecology" of his world. Erikson might argue that Frank has reached a developmental crisis and is attempting

to resolve that crisis. Use facts from the case to describe and illustrate both theorists' views. How might these different theories be used to explain Frank's case?

2. Frank is likely in the early part of Erikson's Stage 5, Identity vs. Role Confusion. How would you characterize the way he is resolving this stage? How would Erikson's concept of Community of Life Cycles influence Frank's resolution? What would James Marcia say about Frank's identity status?

Also see "Connecting Across Cases" question 4 and 9, in the Introduction to this book.

CLASS ACTIVITIES

1. Role-play the conversation between Frank and the friend he caught smoking.

2. Role-play a discussion about Frank between Mr. Groban and Ms. Rowe.

3. Role-play a discussion between Frank's parents and Mr. Groban about Frank's academic problems.

RESEARCH SUGGESTION

1. Research the different measures used to assess moral reasoning and moral judgments in adolescents. Speculate on how Frank would have scored on these measures.

READINGS AND RESOURCES

National Middle School Association at www.nmsa.org

This Web site includes various resources, research, and general information related to the education of middle school students.

Coles, R. (1986). *The political life of children.* New York: Houghton Mifflin.

In this book, Coles explores the development of political consciousness and political views in children and adolescents. He interviews children from several countries and examines how they may adopt parents' political views or adopt very different perspectives. Some of the youth in this book could be compared to Frank, or Coles's general observations may be used to reflect on Frank's actions and beliefs.

Hine, L., & Hedlund, D. (1994, October 15). *Solitary and peer group leisure activities of rural adolescents.* Paper presented at the Research Forum of the National Rural Education Association, Tuscaloosa, AL. (ERIC Document Reproduction Service No. ED384481)

This article reports the results of a longitudinal study of the development of rural youth, with a focus on how the rural setting affects both their school-based and leisure activities and poses transportation problems that contribute to social isolation.

Thoma, S., & Rest, J. (1999). The relationship between moral decision making and patterns of consolidation and transition in moral judgment development. *Developmental Psychology, 35*(2), 323–334.

This study uses both cross-sectional and longitudinal samples to examine whether youths' moral judgments follow Kohlberg's model during periods of either transition or consolidation. The results may shed light on whether Kohlberg's model accurately reflects Frank's level of moral development.

NINE

TALISHA

Overcoming Loss With a New Family

————◆•●•◆————

PRIMARY AND SECONDARY ISSUES

Primary Issues:	Secondary Issues:
• Death of parent, guardianship assumed by neighbor • Effect of maternal addiction to cocaine • Single-parent family • Support systems, extended family and neighbors • Academic motivation	• Sibling relationships • Attachment • Religion • Educational reform and low-income schools • Middle school education

CASE

"I call her Mom because she has taken care of me for such a long time." This is the way 13-year-old Talisha, a bright-eyed African American girl, describes her guardian, Barbara Williams. This is no surprise to Barbara, who says with a smile that Talisha "totally relates to me as her mom." Talisha's biological mother, Monique Stewart, was addicted to crack when Talisha was born. Her addiction overlapped her pregnancy, causing Talisha to be born "positive," according to Barbara. Talisha was the second girl that Monique had, and she later gave birth to two more children, a boy and a girl, who have different fathers.

Barbara explains that during Talisha's early years, she lived with various family members in the large southeastern city where she was born, as her biological mother struggled with her addiction. Talisha's father was often absent and seemed unable to care for her on his own. Her maternal grandmother took Talisha home from the hospital and frequently was the caregiver for her, her three siblings, and several cousins. Barbara was actually a neighbor of Talisha's grandmother. Pregnant at the time, Barbara often found herself caring for Talisha.

> At first, I was just a neighbor. I just came to know her grandmother. Her grandmother had lots of children living with her. She would bring [Talisha] over to my house to visit and then [the grandmother] kinda disappeared and I just started taking care of Talisha. Over time, it became a relationship where I cared for her informally and then became very attached to her, knowing that her mother and father could not care for her. I cared for her as if she was my own child because she brought something special into my life. I was pregnant at the time and it was kind of a preparation for being a mother. It was like a whole different world to me getting to know her, getting attached to her, and getting to love her and having her get attached to me.

Talisha spent a significant part of her childhood with Barbara and Barbara's son, Nile, even while her biological mother was still alive. "Even when [Talisha] returned to her family, I was never not a part of her life. She would spend weekends and major holidays with us." This continued until the death of Talisha's biological mother. "Her mother passed away about five years ago. It was really hard because she had just begun to develop a relationship with her." Barbara says that "Talisha remembers her [biological mom] being sick." Talisha recalls the death as being very difficult, although she is somewhat uncertain about the details of it. "She died about five years ago, I think. I was 10 or maybe 7. It was really hard. I was crying," says Talisha. Further, she says that it was hard on her little brother and sister. "It was sad for them, but I helped my little brother and sister." Barbara agrees that Talisha "has special memories of her younger brother and sister and taking care of them."

After her mother's death, Talisha lived for several years with Barbara and Nile, next door to her grandmother. Although she was a single parent, over time Barbara took on the responsibility of raising Talisha as well. As Barbara recounts, "Basically what happened is that her grandmother could not care for Talisha the way she wanted. She did not have anyone to help her and give her what she needed to keep the kids together. There was no system involved and no money involved. It was just me making the decision to care for Talisha."

Not long after the death of Talisha's biological mother, Barbara (to be referred to hereafter as Mom, in accordance with Talisha's wishes) moved Talisha and her son Nile from the large urban city where they lived to the state capital, a midsized urban community where they have lived for the last five years. The move away from her biological family and the city she called home was not easy for Talisha. The members of her biological family are now spread across several cities in different states. Talisha's older sister lives in another state with her "auntie's friend." Her younger brother and sister still live in the city where Talisha grew up, although they live with different grandparents because they have different fathers. Talisha's biological father lives in the same city as her younger siblings. According to Mom, "when we go down to the area where [the younger siblings and the father] live, we try to see them so that she can keep in contact with them. She knows where they are." When asked if she misses her sisters and brother, Talisha says, "It's okay. It's good, but I miss them." Her mom concurs. "[Talisha] has a sister and brother who do not live with her, which has been one of the most difficult things because she had really grown attached to her siblings."

Talisha's new home in the capital with Mom and Nile is an apartment in a predominantly African American area of the city. One of the first decisions that had to be made by Mom was to determine what grade Talisha should enter. She had just completed second grade, and the options were to have Talisha repeat second grade or go on to third grade. "When she came to school here, I decided to hold her back. I wasn't sure she was ready for the next grade. I did not want to put extra pressure on her." Her mom was ultimately very happy with this decision. "The teacher for the first year at the new school was kind and nurturing." Nile, who is half a year younger than Talisha, was in the same school. "Talisha cried when she realized that Nile was not going to be in the same classroom."

Talisha characterizes her relationship with Nile as "very special." She says that he is "almost my twin" because they are so close in age and she refers to him as her brother. "They were communicating even before he was born," says Mom. "They are close in age, just seven months apart. She was in his new crib before he was. They share a lot and they get along really fabulously. I can count on one hand the number of times the two of them have fought." Talisha says that she and Nile do not have the sibling conflicts she sees many of her friends having. Mom concurs and says that Talisha doesn't know "about that" (referring to sibling rivalries). "Talisha is a peacemaker and [Nile] is pretty laid back. She is older, but because of so many ups and downs in her life, she has been shy and withdrawn. [Talisha and Nile] take on different roles at different times. She would be behind him and then he would be behind her," says Mom, referring to their support of each other.

Talisha further explains, "No, me and my brother, we have had like one or two arguments. Everywhere he goes, I go, and everywhere I go, he goes. He takes care of me. Like if a boy touches me or something he would say 'get off my sister.'" Even when they play basketball, a favorite game of both kids, they get along very well. Talisha loves basketball and is an outstanding player whose quick movements allow her to maneuver past the opposition. On the court she is focused and determined. She was the only girl on her elementary school basketball team. "[The boys] hate it when my brother and I are on the same team because we are good and we do, like, these crazy passes to each other." Recently, Talisha played by herself against three boys her age for a talent show at her school and won. Her friends have nicknamed her "Dunky Cheese" to honor her basketball skills. She describes herself as "not a wild person . . . but I'm moving all the time. Sometimes I play basketball in the house and bounce the ball against the wall. We play football in the house and then we catch the ball and then I tackle [Nile]."

Talisha and Nile also share a love for PlayStation 2. They have "lots of games, like about 21." She recognizes how expensive these games are, and she and Nile often pool their allowance to buy discount games. "The new ones are about $50 and I don't really like the new ones because they get old. I can buy the cheap ones for about $7."

Talisha views herself as an all around good athlete. "I play all kinds of things. I play soccer, baseball, football, and tennis. I'm also a good runner. I ran for the Field and Track team at my elementary school." Talisha competed in the 40-yard dash and "I was the fastest girl in my school." She also competed in the long jump; "you know, that jump thing."

With friends, Talisha says that she likes playing sports, but also likes just talking about a lot of things. "Like one is boys. We talk about who is cute and stuff like that. We talk about how we saw a boy walk by and how cute he was." When something is really bothering Talisha she talks to her mom. "Because I know she will listen to me. She works with kids and I know she will listen." As a single mother, Mom does work full time for a not-for-profit organization whose mission is to help children and advocate for their needs. "Yeah, that's why I can talk to her. Because she has had a lot of experience working with kids."

When Talisha first moved in, Mom says that she showed some hyperactivity, a problem seen often in children born to mothers addicted to crack. "She had a lot of energy and a lot of anger, so she couldn't take criticism at one time or she would get upset or frustrated." One elementary school teacher also noted that Talisha seemed very protective of friends and very sensitive to any action or comment she perceived as an attack on a friend. Although Talisha was never diagnosed or treated, the problems seemed to abate. Mom believes that Talisha "worked through that for herself." Now Mom says Talisha is someone who looks out for others.

> She is kind and on the playground she is known as a real advocate for others. I mean, she won't back down. She has come a long way in that area. We had some problems initially; I guess that is pretty typical of kids who have issues like she does.

Mom says that Talisha will often bring other children home from the playground for dinner.

> If something is wrong on the playground she will bring people to the home to eat dinner and those kinds of things. She just picked up those things on her own. Both the kids have a lot of friends, but many of them come over to see Talisha. My son has a great personality, but the kids just flock to her.

In addition to being kind, Mom describes Talisha as being "one of the most generous and caring [kids] . . . not selfish." Mom is surprised that despite the obstacles Talisha has faced, she has been able to develop such a personality. "For a child living with her family like she did and really lacking stability, it is amazing. It's almost like the opposite of what you think she would be. She really cares." Talisha also believes that volunteering is important, and says, "I worked the gardens at my school and it is important to volunteer."

Mom says that Talisha's caring for others is apparent not only at home but in school as well. "When I talk to teachers over the years, they say she is a real peacemaker." Talisha says that she and her friends do not fight or have many disagreements. When they do, they just find a way to work it out. Talisha describes one situation where she and her brother were having a fight with a local boy.

> My brother was fighting with him and I, like, fought with him too because he was fighting with my brother. But then it was over; we became friends. I said, "Are you okay?" I said, "Let's forget about all of this," and we did. And then we started to play basketball.

Like other teenagers, Talisha enjoys reading and watching television. Her favorite shows are *That's So Raven* and *Sister, Sister.* Her favorite characters on *Sister, Sister* are the twin girls, Tamera and Tia. She says that "they remind me of my cousin Davonna and me acting silly like that." She and Davonna have a close relationship. They are both 13 years old, and while Davonna lives in another state, she often visits in the summer and they get to spend special time together. Davonna is an outgoing and friendly girl with whom Talisha really enjoys spending time.

Talisha sometimes watches MTV, but especially likes to watch her favorite WNBA team, the L.A. Sparks, compete. Her favorite player is Lisa Leslie, whose picture she proudly exhibits on her bedroom wall. "She is good and she is so tall. When I grow up I want to be a WNBA player or a veterinarian." Her mom believes that both are achievable goals for Talisha. The WNBA player comes from "her strong basketball skills" and the veterinarian comes from her "caring about others." Talisha adds that she loves animals and enjoys taking care of her pet hamster.

A book Talisha recently read was called *Slam. Slam* is about a "kid who had a hard time in math, but loved to play basketball. The main character in the book really wants to play basketball, but the principal said, 'You can't play basketball unless your math grades go up.' I really liked him. He really tried."

Struggling in math is something to which Talisha can relate. Mom says that Talisha has done okay in school. "The biggest [difficulty] is math. She has proven that she can overcome obstacles because she has studied and improved her math grades."

According to Talisha, her teachers have often taken the extra time to help her in math. In fact, she really likes science and math and says, "I used to struggle with math, but I stepped up a bit. . . . [Two teachers] encouraged me to do better and my mom encourages me a lot." There is a family rule about studying and doing homework. Even though Mom works full time, she will call home when Talisha and Nile return from school. Talisha says, "Mom will, like, go turn the television off. Even if I tell her I can work with it on she says, 'Turn it off.'" Talisha does not have trouble with reading or most other subjects, but she does not like social studies. "It's hard and I just couldn't understand some things." However, Mom says that Talisha has persevered. This year she worked so hard in social studies that she got a "four on a big test and she was thrilled." (Four is the highest possible grade on this practice exam for advanced placement.) Her high grade is especially impressive because students in her school often do poorly on standardized tests. Fewer than 40% of students at her school achieved a passing grade on recent statewide assessments.

Talisha has a clear idea of what makes a good teacher. Her favorite teachers "would stay after school and spent time with me and explained it to me better." She also likes the teachers who "showed respect for us. They show respect and the kids listen." One time Talisha had a teacher whom she "did not like." When asked why she did not like the teacher, Talisha explains:

> She would crack on kids. She cracked on them. Like on the slow kids. She one time called us the dumbest class she had, and she would even crack on the kids in the other classes. She would call kids fat and stuff like that.

For the most part, Talisha describes her elementary school with fondness. She has just graduated from the sixth grade and will be leaving for a new middle school. The principal at the elementary school "knew my name and so did most of the teachers and I really liked that." Her sixth-grade teacher, Ms. Pacino, said that Talisha's commitment to learning and working hard made her a valuable class member. She observed that during group activities, Talisha often helped other students stay focused on the assignments. "She would tell her group members, 'Here is what we need to do. Let's get this done.'" She also likes to make people laugh and is not afraid to make herself look silly. After a recent science activity involving cotton balls and pipe cleaners, Talisha asked if she could keep three of the colored cotton balls. At lunch she created a hilarious face by taping the cotton balls to her eyebrows and nose and wiggling them as she spoke. Friends report that Talisha is also always singing soft, sweet songs that reflect her nature.

Ms. Pacino says that Talisha does best in school when she can ask questions and interact with others. During an assessment of listening skills where no questions were permitted, Ms. Pacino says that Talisha was "having trouble following directions and just gave up. I think she could have completed the task if more interaction was allowed. But the test directions were very inflexible."

While Talisha likes school, there are some things that she says would make her school better. "I would first fix the inside. The walls are cracking and the ceiling is breaking down. Especially when it rains or something, it leaks." Talisha says that the classes are pretty crowded. "One time I had about 30 kids and my mom got me into a different class." She says that there are about three or four computers in each class, "but we don't use them a lot. Sometimes we play on it or sometimes we get to do our work on them but not a lot." The problems in Talisha's school are frequently issues in urban school districts, especially those in low-income neighborhoods funded primarily through local property taxes. Talisha's school has a high percentage of students from low-income families, with over 90% receiving some type of public assistance.

Mom has some real concerns about Talisha's upcoming middle school experience. The three middle schools in their city are all failing to meet state standards. So even though the No Child Left Behind legislation allows parents to choose any middle school, in reality "there is no choice," says Mom.

> I can send her to any of the middle schools, but they are failing. I have a choice, but they are failing choices. I always thought it was all about the kids. But I know that the schools don't have adequate books, teaching materials, and not every parent can send their child to private school, so I will likely pick Harrison Middle School. I have not been pleased with it for my son. He is in the honors program, but I'm not happy with the way the staff interacted. They can shut kids down versus bringing out the best in them and not challenge them enough.

When asked whether she wants to attend the public school or go to private school if she has the chance, Talisha says,

> I want to go to both. I want to go to the one that is going to be better for me. I don't want to go somewhere where kids are playing around because then you might start playing around . . . No, I don't want to be in classes where kids are playing around.

The desire for a private education goes beyond the concerns about the local public middle schools. Talisha and her mom would embrace a religious education if they could find a way to pay the tuition. According to Mom,

> [Religion] has had an impact on [Talisha] and me . . . As a single parent, I have had to overcome some obstacles and struggles. For the five years we have been in this area, religion has knitted us together as a family. I have a

standard. We pray together as a family and we talk about [religion] at dinner. It is not forced on the children. It was not forced on [Talisha], she grew into it. She likes it. She likes the church where we attend because they don't push their values. It is very nurturing and loving, and it is about giving and not receiving. So it's not that she is taught 'do, do, do' and 'don't, don't, don't.' That's Mommy's job. I say that stuff to her. I tell her that she has to know that certain things have certain consequences. She knows that religion is very important to me. She sees me reading and sees magnets on my refrigerator [referring to religious materials]. She sees me teaching at our church and working with the youth and that [religion] is a value of mine. It has helped her. It is a confidence builder. She listens to the scripture that tells you that you can do all things through Christ's strength. She knows that. She knew that with math.

Like Mom, Talisha believes that religion has played an important role in her life. She says,

Because I was, like, not so great. But I went to church and learned about respect and I wanted to be good. You know that I don't curse at all because I learned that it is wrong. . . . When Pastor talks, we listen. She is so nice and so is her husband. They really care. . . . We get to play basketball and they buy food and stuff for us.

Mom also emphasizes the strong sense of community at their church.

Our pastor is wonderful. She and her husband have done so much for the children of our community. Talisha is at church several days a week. The only days she does not go to church are on Saturday and Thursday. On the other days there is always some activity to involve the children.

In many ways, the church community has become an extended family for Talisha. According to Mom, "this is what [Talisha] needed because when she lived with her family she lived with a lot more people. My family unit alone is much smaller and it took a lot for her to adjust to it."

Religion has also provided Talisha with strength to deal with her fears. "I worry something will happen to my family. I don't want anything bad to happen to me or my family, but I believe in God and He won't let anything bad happen to us." Talisha still has some worries about the future. It makes her sad to think about people dying. "Like when family members are sick, I'm afraid that they are going to die. That would make me sad . . . . I don't want my family to die so fast."

Despite some fears about what the future holds, Talisha has her heart set on her goals. She will either be a veterinarian or a WNBA player. Mom just wants her to

> get a good education, be successful, and be able to make a difference. She is already making a difference in people's lives. Some kids don't like themselves and they are growing up with so many issues, and they get to adulthood and they haven't resolved their issues and have wasted lives. I don't want to see that happen to her. I want her to know that no matter what is in her family history or her background, or what I might not be able to offer her, or what she doesn't have, that she is a whole and complete individual and has a lot to offer. I believe that she will be successful. She is driven.

Ms. Pacino says that Talisha seeks out ways to move toward her dreams. During a recent goal-setting activity in class, Talisha identified three subgoals to help her reach her dreams: get good grades in math and science classes, win an athletic scholarship to help her go to college, and play basketball in college while she studies courses that will help her get into veterinary school. With the continued support of Mom and her own motivation to succeed, Talisha may just be the first WNBA player to be a brilliant veterinarian.

DISCUSSION QUESTIONS

1. Research suggests that extended family and friends often provide an important support network for children from low-income families. Discuss how Talisha's support network has helped her to overcome the potential problems she might have experienced as a child of a parent with a crack addiction.

2. Talisha and her mom have many positive things to say about her teachers but are critical of the school and school system. How does this case illustrate the types of problems that are typical of schools in low-income areas? How are the teachers in Talisha's school helping her to overcome potential learning problems that may be rooted in her chaotic early home environment?

3. How would you characterize the parenting style of Talisha's mom (Barbara Williams)? How does she promote positive cognitive and emotional development in Talisha?

APPLYING THEORETICAL PERSPECTIVES

1. Talisha's early years were unstable and included moving around to different homes. How would most attachment theorists predict that this would influence a child's emotional development? Using Erikson's theory, how would you explain the fact that Talisha has been able to develop positive emotional relationships?

2. Albert Bandura argues that observational learning is a powerful influence on behavior. What in Talisha's case could be used by Bandura to support his theory? Use specific examples from the case.

RESEARCH SUGGESTIONS

1. No Child Left Behind legislation is the subject of much debate in the educational and political communities. Under this legislation, what are the options for parents whose children attend a school district where all middle schools are failing? What changes do you think are needed in this legislation, or other educational policies, to address the problem identified by Talisha's mom—that she effectively has no real choice in schools?

2. Research the short- and long-term effects of maternal cocaine addiction and prenatal exposure to cocaine on children's cognitive, emotional, and physical development. Report on programs that address the needs of both parents addicted to drugs and their children.

3. Form a group to research the issues of foster parenting and adoption. Investigate how decisions are typically made regarding foster care and adoption. In class, discuss reasons why Barbara Williams may have been reluctant to pursue legal adoption of Talisha. What potential problems might she face as Talisha's caregiver?

CLASS ACTIVITIES

1. Role-play the conversation where Talisha's mom informed Talisha of the death of her biological mother. What would be the most effective way to deliver this news to a child in middle childhood? What possible emotional or behavioral reactions might you see?

2. Working in groups, use a visual format to analyze the microsystem, mesosystem, exosystem, and macrosystem influences on Talisha.

READINGS AND RESOURCES

McEntire, N. (2003). *Children and grief.* ERIC Clearinghouse on Elementary and Early Childhood Education. (ERIC Document Reproduction Service No. ED475393)

This ERIC Digest discusses children's reactions to the loss of a loved one and ways in which parents and teachers can help grieving children.

Scholzman, S. (2003). The pain of losing a parent. *Educational Leadership, 60*(8), 91–92.

This article focuses on the emotional effects of a parent's death on children and ways in which teachers can help.

Brooks, S. (2002). Kinship and adoption. *Adoption Quarterly, 5*(3), 55–66.

This article discusses kinship networks common in caring for African American children and how traditional adoption networks often discourage adoption by family members or friends.

Gibbs, P., & Muller, U. (2000). Kinship foster care moving to the mainstream: Controversy, policy, and outcomes. *Adoption Quarterly, 4*(2), 57–87.

This article examines the increases in kinship care and examines differences in foster care by kin and nonkin.

O'Donnell, K., et al. (1994). *The infant care project: A mother-child intervention model directed at cocaine use during pregnancy. Final report.* Durham, NC: Duke University Medical Center. (ERIC Document Reproduction Service No. ED408814)

This report discusses intervention programs for mothers dealing with cocaine addiction problems and for their children.

Suchman, N. (2002). Maternal addiction, child maladjustment, and socio-demographic risks: Implications for parenting behaviors. *Addiction, 95*(9), 1417–1428.

This article examines interactions between mothers with drug addictions and their infants and reports research on children's developmental problems associated with maternal addiction.

Barone, D. (1994). Myths about crack babies. *Educational Leadership, 52*(2), 67–68.

This article reviews research on problems experienced by children prenatally exposed to crack and dispels myths about what teachers might expect to see in their behavior.

TEN

ELENA

Surviving Family Problems

————◆•◆•◆————

PRIMARY AND SECONDARY ISSUES

Primary Issues:	*Secondary Issues:*
• Adolescent identity development—especially with respect to peers, career choice, family relationships, dating, ethnicity, and conflicts with authorities • Friendship, peer relationships, and ethnic conflicts • The effects of alcoholism on the family	• Physical self-concept and body image • Domestic violence • Motivation and school achievement • Teacher and student relationships • Problems faced by gay, lesbian, and bisexual students and how schools address these problems

CASE

Elena arrives for class early and immediately consults with Mr. Quinn, her journalism teacher. She asks him several questions but then seems sure of her plans. As the 16-year-old editor of an award-winning student newspaper for a 3,000 student urban high school, she has confidence in her writing and her ideas. She writes all of the paper's editorials, and Mr. Quinn notes that Elena does not shy away from difficult topics.

> I think her main strength is that she is pretty fearless. She is fearless in writing, at least. She gets an idea in her head and she goes straight ahead with it. That's also one of her weaknesses. She tends to just get this thought in her head and then just go, go, go. And it's not at all organized. She really would benefit from some organizational processes. She doesn't like to be told that she should pre-write, that she should outline articles. She doesn't like to be told that she can't just sit down and dash it off and have it be perfect. Eventually she will just be able to sit down and dash it off and it will be fine, but now, now is not that time. Especially because she tends to pick topics that are tough.

Mr. Quinn is trying to help Elena with organizational skills so that she can focus her writing, but he wants her to maintain her strong spirit. Elena has told Mr. Quinn about her past personal struggles with her father's alcoholism and violence toward her mother, who is currently seeking a divorce. He knows that courage has been essential to her survival as well as her success as a writer, so he encourages her to express herself in ways that will get people to listen.

One of Elena's editorials, which was nominated for a city-wide award, discussed issues faced by gay, lesbian, and bisexual students at her high school and what seemed to be administrative efforts to delay the formation of a Tolerance Club. She interviewed more than 20 gay, lesbian, and bisexual students for the article and with advice from Mr. Quinn, cited the school's Vision Statement as support for her arguments that the club should be formed. Elena described why she chose this topic from the list of topics presented for the competition.

> It was either gays and lesbians, zero tolerance, or sex education. Zero tolerance we hear about every day in the newspaper. Pretty boring, I think. And sex education wasn't really a good match for me. It wasn't important because I'm not taking sex ed or anything. And then gays and lesbians, I was like, "Oh maybe I could do that." I like controversy. I like when people talk about my articles. I really do. And if I have to write about something, it should take somebody's attention, which is the point of writing. You have to attract

people in to read your articles. So I wrote something that I thought most people would read. Because even though there are a lot of homophobes out there, they have to understand that [gays, lesbians, and bisexuals] are all around. There was, like, 20 students that came out of the closet [while she was writing the article], I mean, that I knew of, and there are still more out there.

The editorial described the experiences of gay and lesbian students at the school and argued that it was time to support formation of a Tolerance Club. The editorial provoked a strong reaction from the principal, who was not interviewed and who felt Mr. Quinn should have let her preview it. However, following some pressure from the district office, the club was finally formed. While not involved with the club, Elena was delighted with student response to her article and upset with the principal's reaction.

I think [the principal] didn't get past reading the title itself, *As Gay as Gay Can Be.* I meant as happy as the gay people can be. I didn't mean as gay as the gay can really be. You know, I was trying to make a point, and if she can't get past it, then obviously she does not deserve to be a principal for her students or gays.

(Note: the editorial is included at the end of this case.) Elena works hard for teachers when she has a good relationship with them. She has earned high marks from an English teacher said to be one of the school's most demanding and rigorous teachers. Elena admires the teacher's high standards and expectations.

[She] prepares us for college instead of being just a high school teacher. . . . You know how some teachers are just like fun, work, or no fun at all. She's really into the teaching of it. She actually spends time on our work; she corrects our mistakes and . . . we tend to learn from those mistakes, and from other people's mistakes when she tells us about them.

Elena also admires the way teachers like Mr. Quinn make schoolwork enjoyable.

He is real cool. . . . I think he taught me how to write . . . because you actually learn in his class. You know, it's fun and you learn, but there are times where you have to be serious, and that's how you mature in class.

However, Elena has had conflicts with several of her teachers. Mr. Quinn, who often advises Elena about school, points out that if Elena does not respect a teacher, "she doesn't do the work unless the inspiration hits her. She does the work when she either feels like doing the work or when she actually has to do the work." Elena is critical of her French teacher's teaching methods and has been thrown out of her class several times.

> All she does is tell us to do the work. She writes it on the board, and she speaks French. And she obviously should know that we don't know French. I mean, we are in a French class to learn French. All she does is make us repeat words. She doesn't help in class. So she's really bad, . . . all the kids are just, like, joking around. She has a bad temper too. And it makes us want to laugh and make her even more mad.

Elena is currently failing French and will have to repeat the course in summer school or night school unless she brings her grade up. But Elena does not seem to want to make that effort. If schoolwork does not interest her, she sometimes simply refuses to do it.

Ironically, Elena's family is Puerto Rican and she speaks Spanish fluently. However, she took French because she did not want to take a two-hour exam on a Saturday to get credit for Spanish. "I'm not going to give up two hours of my Saturday just to take a test. I'd rather sleep." She also failed physics because she was tardy for this first period class 30 times. Her current grade point average is around 2.0, and she has four semester course credits to make up before she graduates. Family difficulties may have contributed to Elena's academic problems. Throughout her high school years, her parents had marital problems. They decided to separate over a year ago and began seeing other persons, but both continued to live with Elena in a six-room apartment. Elena, who did most of her schoolwork on a computer in the living room, does not cite this as a reason for her poor grades, but Mr. Quinn says he can't imagine how a young teen like Elena could cope with the daily tension and conflict that pervaded this household.

Mr. Quinn points out that despite her bravado in writing, Elena often comes across as self-conscious and unsure of herself. He attributes much of her insecurity to her relationship with her father, who was drunk on his only visit to the school.

> Her father has put a lot of things on her over the years. And he is always taking it out on her and her mother for what he has perceived as his own inadequacies. But he doesn't want to admit that they are his own inadequacies, so he puts it on Elena and he puts it on her mother. . . . [During his trip to school] he was being boisterously proud of [Elena]. And you could see from the way she reacted that she was not at all comfortable. It seemed sort of like she

didn't believe him. Like she knew that he was just putting on a show for the teacher, to show that he could be a good father.

Elena's parents came to the United States from Puerto Rico after graduating from high school. They moved from New Jersey to a large midwestern city and initially lived in a neighborhood that was plagued with gang problems. Elena said she never felt safe in her old neighborhood. When she was seven, the family moved to an apartment in a more stable working class area. When she was younger, Elena said that the family was close and did many things together. However, problems between her parents were apparent even in those early years. Her mother got involved in a Christian church and bible studies, while her father, who worked as a tow truck driver, began drinking. As a young child, Elena says she felt closer to her father than her mother, who used to hit her and her brother to make sure that their misbehavior did not anger their father. "My dad would just scream at us and we would just get scared by that and we would, like, freeze up. My Mom would have to hit us." As the father's drinking increased, he became violent, and Elena's mother had to protect her children. When Elena was five, her father

kidnapped me and my brother and he took us into a car after he busted my mom's head with a bottle, a beer bottle. And I had called the police before he dragged us out. We had just learned how to call 911 that day from school and how to tell the operator what was going on, so I picked up the phone and told them that my dad hit my mom, and then my dad dragged me and my brother into his car. And then my mom had to drag me out. I mean, she ran out even with her head busted and she, she tried dragging me out and my brother, but I was closer to the door. My dad ran over my foot as he drove off.

For many years, her father's unpredictable behavior created a chaotic family environment. He frequently accused his wife of cheating on him and once broke her wrist. Elena was usually the one who called the police or intervened to protect her mother. He sometimes tried to blame her for his problems by saying, "Oh, you really don't love me because you called the police." But Elena replied, "Okay, if you acted like a man maybe I wouldn't have to call the police." She says that she educated herself about alcoholism over the years by reading books and finding resources from Web sites of national organizations dealing with alcoholism. This helped her to understand the need to avoid enabling her father's destructive behaviors.

Several years ago, her mother drew up divorce papers, but the minister of her Christian church convinced her to try to work out the problems. However, her father's violence and alcohol problems continued and her mother gave up trying to reconcile. In the past year, Elena's mother filed for divorce and obtained a restraining order against her husband. However, he did not move out of the apartment until about one month ago. Elena says her mother has always done her best to provide for the family and make up for the problems caused by her husband's drinking and violent behavior. Despite her husband's objections, she obtained an associate's degree and now works as a family educator at a center for women recovering from alcohol or drug addiction. Elena's father, who is 35 years old, had a heart attack last year and later had his car taken away following an arrest for driving under the influence of alcohol. He has since started going to Alcoholics Anonymous meetings.

Elena does recall some happy times with her father, mother, and younger brother, especially during trips to visit her father's large family estate in Puerto Rico or to Disney World in Florida. But she says things are much better now that he is gone. She has developed such a close relationship with her mother that she calls her "my sister." They shop together, try out new hairstyles, encourage each other, and share everything.

Their apartment is bright and cheerful with a well-organized space set aside for Elena's computer and schoolwork. Although the location, near a major city highway, makes it noisy at times, the high ceilings and well-kept older furniture give it a sense of subdued elegance. On this spring day it is warm but airy and immaculately clean.

Elena's mom is a very pretty woman who looks youthful but tired as she reflects on her difficult marriage. She was born in Brooklyn but finished high school in Puerto Rico, where she met her husband. They moved first to New Jersey but settled in the midwest after a vacation there. She is currently dating a detective, whom Elena likes. She carefully monitors all of Elena's activities, friendships, and dating relationships, and Elena says that she feels she can talk with her mother about anything. Mom takes pride in Elena's skills in using the computer and writing and knows which classes and teachers she likes. Despite some difficulties with English, Mom goes to school to pick up Elena's report cards and has met several of her teachers. She knew about Elena's conflicts with certain teachers and with the principal and voices strong support for her daughter. However, she emphasizes that her daughter must also take responsibility for her actions.

> Sometimes it's like a teacher says something to her, and she talks back to the teacher. So I don't know if it's about a problem [with the teacher] or

anger that she has with some things. I don't know, but she will have to work on her attitude.

Mom values education both for herself and her daughter. She hopes to complete a bachelor's degree someday and encourages Elena to concentrate on her studies rather than on dating boys. "I don't want her to get married yet. She should finish high school and continue. First, an associates degree and then a bachelors, and then a doctorate degree." Most importantly, she advises Elena that she can rise above her family's problems.

> I always talk to her about how when I was her age [pause] like the problems that we have here today. [pause] I went to high school and my father was an alcoholic too. And I passed all the problems, and then I have my associates degree. And she can do it too. I say that to her. That is life. Even if she has problems, she can make it.

Elena expresses admiration for her mother's hard work and resourcefulness. "Yes, she's had a lot of jobs. I don't know. She doesn't speak the perfect English, but she's had some job experiences where, wow! You know, sometimes I'm, like, 'How did you do that?' She gets around really fast." Mom admits that she likes to feel she can make it on her own.

> Sometimes [Elena] tries to correct me, my English [she laughs]. She will say, "Mom, no. We have to sit down, and I'm going to teach you how to say this." I don't need that. I go with my English whatever place I want to go and work.

The church has been an important source of support for both Elena and her mother. They have attended several different Pentecostal Christian churches and currently attend different churches. Mom says that church is important because "I feel safe there. It's like when you go inside the church you feel, like, free. Your mind is not thinking about your problems."

Elena emphasizes that the pastor is important in her choice of a church. She left one church where the pastor's problems were dividing the congregation. Based on the recommendations of friends, she began attending another church where she feels safe and comfortable. Elena describes the people at her church as

> always, always there for me. I can call up a friend, and they're always there for me. They're cool. It's usually the youth. You know, and if not the youth, the pastors. . . . They're my second family, and my best friends altogether.

She met her current boyfriend, Jose, through the church, although she says that she is taking the relationship really slowly. She had previously dated a boy who seemed nice at first but later proved very immature. For awhile she and her mother argued over her dating him because Mom thought he took advantage of Elena's generous nature by having her pay for his phone bills. Elena said that she realized he "reminded me of my father" and finally ended the relationship after figuring out for herself that her mother was right. Jose, however, respects her wishes and even asked to meet her father. That impressed Elena because "no one had ever asked to meet my dad." Also, her mother has met and approved of Jose. Still, Elena is reluctant to say that she is in love and prefers to call it puppy love. "I don't want to fall in love yet. I don't want to get hurt."

Elena attends church and school with one of her lifelong best friends, Sheri. She and Sheri grew up together and went to the same babysitter. They had conflicts along the way, including one time when they did not talk for a full year following a disagreement that Elena and Sheri cannot remember now. Elena also works on the school paper with Sheri, against whom she competed for the position of editor.

Elena: [Mr. Quinn] asked who wanted to run for minor things like news, news editor, sports editor, and all that stuff. And I wanted to be editor-in-chief, but they said that you had to be a senior. And I was, like, aww, I'm a junior. So I asked Mr. Quinn and he was, like, that's fine. So I ran and I was running against Sheri, my best friend, you know, and Willie, who was another senior. They were both seniors, and he told us to bring, like, a speech or something so we could persuade them. So I wrote my paper, I spent 20 minutes on my computer trying to figure something out. I felt pretty good, and not only did I persuade them, I made fun of the other ones. . . . I was making fun of Willie because they call him silly Willie. I was, like, 'You guys don't want a silly editor; you really want a serious editor.' Mr. Quinn said that it was pretty obvious who was going to win. I knew I was going to win, but I didn't want to say anything [both laugh]. There was no competition, I guess.

Interviewer: And Sheri was, you were still able to be friends after that?

Elena: Yes, of course. . . . I mean that same night that we were working on our speech, I called her, and I'm, like, 'What are you going to write?' Because we are so much alike, I didn't want to write the same thing that she wrote. So, she told me what she wrote and I wrote the opposite.

Elena says that Sheri is always there for her. "She takes care of me, more than she takes care of herself. She's very caring." One night Elena was afraid to stay home alone with her father, who had been arrested the week before for domestic violence. She called Sheri and another friend, Penny. Both of them came to the house and slept over to make sure that Elena was okay.

Elena's friendship with Penny has also had its ups and downs. "The weird thing about her is that . . . before we met, we were actually enemies." They had gotten into an argument and a fight on a bus, but neither remembered it at first.

> Then I guess I didn't recognize her and she didn't recognize me either until, like, sophomore year. We ended up being really close friends and everything. But she's, like, the only unique friend that I have. Her mom is a lesbian, and she has, like, everything weird. It reminds me of my dad's side of the family. So we're like cousins—cousin friends.

A slender, pretty girl with large brown eyes and thick, curly black hair cascading down her back, Elena sometimes expresses insecurity about her appearance. "I have really bad hair," she laments, "It's nappy"—a trait that she attributes to her grandmother, who was black. Mom said that Elena often gets up an hour early to work on her hair, which she likes to arrange in a variety of creative styles. Elena says she has often been teased with nicknames, such as "Flaca" or skinny, Big Head, and "Nigglet" because of her dark skin. She is also very aware of what she wears and objects to the school's dress code, which requires all students to wear navy pants and white shirts or blouses. Despite these restrictions, she says that kids at school still get teased for the kind of clothes they wear.

> You know, they get picked on for the kind of shoes they wear, the kind of pants they wear. I mean, they're still the same color but there's still certain marks. And they try so hard to figure it out. Umm, are they wearing Old Navy pants or are they wearing Gap. . . . If you wear Old Navy then, okay, you're good enough, you know, and if you don't, then you're not. I mean it's, it's

kind of dumb. I mean, it's really dumb, but it's still happening, and either way, you're still going to get picked on.

Her elementary school was in a neighborhood with many gang problems, and Elena appreciates the safe atmosphere at her high school. However, she does not think the dress code or the school-issued transparent backpacks help to reduce gang problems or teasing from peers. She points out that there are groups in the school who still have conflicts.

> I think here there's a little thing about Puerto Ricans and Mexicans or Puerto Ricans and blacks against the Mexicans. I mean, I have Mexican friends but we, I guess it's a culture thing, I'm not sure what it is. It's like, we don't hate them, but we can't get along with them. I mean, I get along with most of them, but it gets bad after a while. It's, it's, really, I guess it's the way we were brought up. You know, like, stay away from those who aren't your type of people. So I guess Puerto Ricans and blacks are, like, in a group together and then Mexicans and everyone else.

While there have been no gang problems in the school, Elena has heard about problems between youth from the school and outside gangs. One Mexican group called the Aztecas seems to take on a policing function regarding the gangs.

> [The Aztecas] are a group of Mexicans who tend to, like, have fights with real gang bangers. They're just a crew, that's what they called them, a crew. They are always picking on gang bangers, which they are not big enough to do that. You know, they are not a big gang, and that's how they end up getting killed, I mean really. We've had two kids already who got killed.

Some teachers are aware of the ethnic divisions, and the school records information about suspected gang members on confidential parts of student records. But the absence of open conflict in the school keeps the issue at a low profile.

The school's total population includes about 60% Mexican youth, 17% Puerto Rican youth, 8% African American, and another 6% immigrants from Eastern European countries. The school has clubs promoting cultural activities for Latino, African American, and Polish students, and its Web site boasts that its students speak over 40 different languages. While the teachers are mostly Caucasian, many of them make an effort to incorporate aspects of the different cultures of the students into their curriculum. Mr. Quinn, who also teaches American literature, points out that the public school curriculum is rich in

African American literature but contains relatively few Hispanic writers. He brings in additional contemporary Puerto Rican and Mexican writers and says that the students are sometimes surprised to hear that there are writers that represent their cultures. "I had a kid this year in front of the whole class say, 'There are no Puerto Rican writers. We don't like to write.'"

Elena has responded well to Mr. Quinn's cultural sensitivity. She hopes to become a journalist, and her dream is to attend Northwestern University, one of the nation's finest journalism programs. However, given her poor grades, she is beginning to worry about her prospects and her possible inability to pay for further education. In addition, she has found that being editor is a challenge. She likes it "when people look up to me even though they are older than me." However, students do not always do their assignments for the paper, and Elena often ends up writing stories that are not completed. She is eager to leave high school but somewhat fearful of what lies beyond it.

> I wish I could just graduate now, but I can't. But umm, I really, I really, want to graduate and go to college and get a degree or two and major in journalism. But the way things are going, I don't think I'm going to be able to go. [laughs nervously] I think I'm going to cry.

Several of her teachers continue to encourage Elena to believe in her talents, which they say she sometimes underestimates. They hope she will be able to transfer her fearlessness in writing into actions that will help her realize her dreams. Her mother believes that she also needs to learn to control her anger and put her romantic interests on hold. Elena says she is trying. Her mother points out that the principal recently asked her to do an article on sexual harassment for the paper. Elena makes a face, but then she smiles and says, "I already handed it in."

Page 10   **Holmes Times**   **February, 2001**

As Gay as Gay Can Be

by Elena Garcia

This is a new year, a new generation, and a new day and age. Love has been in the air and there is nothing that can stop it! It has taken control of teens all over, even here at Holmes. High school is the number one place where teens socialize and meet new people—people who we learn to care for, trust, and love. This leads to new people becoming couples every year. We see new couples of all sorts, different races, different colors, different beliefs, different styles, even different sexual orientations.

By junior high and high school, students are experimenting and becoming aware of their own sexuality. They are also aware of sexual orientation issues, both in the personal and political sphere. Sexual preference is made an issue daily by certain school activities, such as dances and other social events, and by cultural influences.

Some may be disturbed while others might not be disturbed by it, but gay teens of all sorts are "coming out of the closet" and there is nothing that can stop them. Rick Diego, a straight high school student, says, "The bi, gay, and lesbian [students] are no different from the straight. . . . Many fail to realize that they are like any other, for they are human. It's not a disability to choose one's own persona. Like one who is straight chooses how he or she likes to get down, so does one who is bi, gay, or lesbian. And when dealing with society they are as equal and as well-qualified to perform duties and responsibilities as the next man or woman. In the classroom, in the office, or out in society, they are just as wise and intelligent as any other." I strongly agree with Rick's point of view: It isn't a disability to be yourself, I see the disability as not being able to express yourself.

It may surprise you that some gay, lesbian, and bisexual students are or were representing Holmes in extracurricular activities or outstanding academic performances. They truly are everywhere, and these students have the right to be who they want to be. They are taking advantage of this right by being open with their family members and friends.

Over a dozen gay, lesbian, and bisexual students were interviewed here at Holmes for this article. Some were willing to lend their names to this article, but because not everyone is as accepting as their friends and parents, their comments will be kept anonymous.

A male bisexual student here at Holmes said, "I am not ashamed of being bisexual, I know all my friends and teachers love me for me and I don't regret who I am. I have better grades than some straight students do; my sexual orientation shouldn't really matter." When asked if she was ever picked on for her sexual orientation, another bisexual student said, "Some students pick on me because of my sexuality, but I guess they're just going to have to face it."

School isn't the only place where people have trouble facing gay and lesbian students. When asked when he came out of the closet and if his parents know, a gay student here at Holmes stated, "Well, I haven't come out of the closet. Some people know, but only my closest friends. My parents do not know. I don't think I could tell them."

It is disappointing how students cannot even be themselves even at home. It is sad to know what any person is likely to do because of people who do not accept them. The Gay and Lesbian Community Center's (GLCC) statistics show that gay and lesbian youth are at least three times more likely than heterosexual youth to attempt suicide.

One reason behind this fact is that gay, lesbian, and bisexual students feel isolated. Gay, lesbian, and bisexual student alliances on some campuses have helped to alleviate this. On other campuses they will have to fight their way in, as religious clubs and others have had to do.

In the past, students have been frustrated in their attempts to establish a student alliance here at Holmes. They were told that they needed a faculty sponsor and were hesitant to approach any faculty member for help.

This year, a group of students found a sponsor and circulated petitions asking for a "Tolerance Club" that would "foster understanding and acceptance of diversity," and "speak out against hate, injustice, racism, sexism, anti-gay jokes, name-calling and persecution." They collected hundreds of student signatures in support of the club.

I believe the school should support the club, too, since the Vision Statement of our School Improvement Plan for Advancing Academic Achievement (SIPAAA) declares, "Holmes High School is committed to providing a multicultural environment by helping students respect and understand diverse racial, ethnic, and social groups."

Society tends to pull some people down for who they are and what they believe. While I am not a lesbian or a bisexual student, I will stand my ground and say that I believe it is time to support tolerance at Holmes. In this new world, as in the old, what happens in schools plays a major role in shaping society. We should all try to not play a part that keeps people from being who they are and expressing their beliefs.

DISCUSSION QUESTIONS

1. What do you consider to be the most important events, relationships, or influences affecting Elena's development? Be ready to support your analysis using concepts, research, and theories from your text.

2. How have alcoholism and domestic violence affected Elena's family and her development? What does research on these two problems suggest might be the effect of her father's alcoholism and domestic violence on Elena? What evidence does the case offer that Elena is or is not successfully coping with these problems? What approaches do you think are needed to help her?

3. What role has friendship played in Elena's life? How do her friendships reflect her level of social and emotional development? How do Elena's social cognitive skills affect her friendships and her role as editor of the school paper?

4. Elena's school performance has been erratic. What factors do you think are responsible for this? Is Elena intrinsically or extrinsically motivated? What types of motivation appear to be most effective for her? How would you describe her ability to self-regulate? If you were one of Elena's teachers, what would you do to encourage Elena to improve her school performance? Support your answer from a research and theoretical perspective.

5. What problems does Elena identify for gay, lesbian, and bisexual students in her editorial? What might you add to her description, based on research on youth who are gay, lesbian, or bisexual? How do tolerance clubs, such as those supported by the Gay, Lesbian, Straight Education Network (see www.glsen.org below), help address problems faced by these youth?

6. Elena is described as "fearless" in her writing, and she has shown considerable strength in confronting her father. Researchers might say she has a strong sense of self-efficacy and an internal locus of control. How would these characteristics help Elena cope with the challenges in her life? What factors might contribute to her sense of self-efficacy or her internal locus of control?

APPLYING THEORETICAL PERSPECTIVES

1. Select two developmental theorists and discuss how they might analyze Elena's social and emotional development.

2. Using the theoretical frameworks provided by Erikson and Marcia, discuss Elena's development of a sense of identity. How well developed is her identity in different areas, such as religious or spiritual values, friendships and peer relationships, romantic relationships, school and career, or family relationships? What factors have influenced her resolution of Erikson's psychosocial crises?

Also see "Connecting Across Cases" question 8, in the Introduction to this book.

CLASS ACTIVITIES

1. Role-play a discussion between Elena and her mother about dating and sexuality.

2. With a partner, role-play a discussion between Elena and Mr. Quinn about her school performance and her goal to study journalism at a top university.

RESEARCH SUGGESTIONS

1. Working with several other students, identify local organizations and resources for families experiencing problems with alcoholism or domestic violence and report to the class on the types of services available.

2. With a partner, research and report on the use of school uniforms as a means of reducing violence, bullying, and teasing in schools.

READINGS AND RESOURCES

Children of alcoholics: Important facts. National Association for Children of Alcoholics at www.nacoa.net/coa3.htm

This Web site provides educational information about alcoholism and resources to support children of alcoholic parents.

National Coalition Against Domestic Violence at www.ncadv.org

This Web site provides up-to-date statistics and research on domestic violence and its impact on families.

Osofsky, J. D. (2003). Prevalence of children's exposure to domestic violence and child maltreatment: Implications for prevention and intervention. *Clinical Child & Family Psychology Review, 6*(3), 161–170.

This article examines the prevalence of domestic violence and the immediate and long-term impact on child and adolescent development. Protective factors that influence developmental outcomes are also discussed.

Sharleen, K. L. (2000). Coats of many colors: Serving the multiracial child and adolescent. *Journal of Family and Consumer Sciences: From Research to Practice, 92*(5), 37–40.

This article examines the identity development of multiracial children and adolescents and provides practical suggestions for fostering positive development.

Gay, Lesbian, Straight Education Network at www.glsen.org

Includes information on gay and lesbian youth, links to school-based clubs, discussion groups and local organizing tools for students, and educational resources, links, and curriculum tools for educators.

U.S. Department of Education. Manual on School Uniforms (2001). www.ed .gov/updates/uniforms.html

This manual discusses school policies on school uniforms and how to implement such policies.

Siegel, L. (1996). *Point of view: School uniforms.* American Civil Liberties Union. Available at archive.aclu.org/congress/uniform.html

This article discusses different points of view and research on the impact of school uniforms.

HECTOR

Talking Through Troubles

———•◦●◦•———

PRIMARY AND SECONDARY ISSUES

Primary Issues:	*Secondary Issues:*
• Resiliency • Teacher-student relationships • Social isolation/ social development • Effects of domestic and community violence on development	• Cultural values • Loss of loved ones/ friends to violence • Depression

CASE

Hector walks across the stage of his high school auditorium carrying his French horn and smiling broadly. He is smartly dressed, all in black, with a gold chain mirroring the glow of his horn. He puts his heart into his music and is proud to be a member of his school band because school has always been one of his major refuges from the deep hurts he has experienced in life.

His difficulties are not apparent on the surface. Ms. Turner, his twelfth-grade English teacher, describes him as

> a party boy, and a friend to everyone. . . . Everybody loves Hector. Even people who don't know him are crazy about him, the girls especially, because he is beguiling and charming. And he's got that, he's got the doe eyes . . . he just plucks your heart strings.

She says he is bright, with a talent for getting right to the heart of an issue, but his school performance has been erratic. He usually manages to complete assignments just before they are due. He shows an ability to think lucidly and write concisely; however, his attendance at school has been so poor that his teachers may be required by school policies to give him failing grades. Ms. Turner senses that there is something beneath his bright surface. "Hector just scares me to death. He just seems to be where trouble is all the time. You know, and he always seems to be running."

Hector's home and neighborhood are the sources of both his troubles and his support. His parents emigrated to the United States from Mexico when Hector was an infant, seeking a better life for their children. Initially, his father went to San Diego to work, and his mother brought him and his older sister to live with her relatives in a large midwestern city. For several years his parents continued their long distance relationship. His father joined the family in the midwest a couple of years later, after Hector's younger brother was born. They moved several times during Hector's early life, always looking for a safer neighborhood for their children. Although their limited English restricted job opportunities, they have both managed to find steady employment. His mother works in a candy factory and his father is a laborer in a steel mill. Several years ago they purchased a two-flat in a neighborhood that included a mix of industrial complexes, single family houses, apartments, and large parks. They currently share the second floor of the two-flat with an aunt and cousin and rent the first floor. Hector says that the neighborhood was good when they first moved in but has recently had problems with gangs.

Despite the frequent moves, Hector has happy memories of his early childhood, playing games with his brother and his friends in the hallway of their apartment building. He also fondly recalls going to the zoo with his mother and his sister. "We used to pack sandwiches and take blankets. We were all on the bus together in the back, just talking. I used to enjoy going to the zoo a lot, seeing the animals, just chilling." He still feels very close to both his brother and sister. Despite a two-year difference in age with his brother, he says that they still have many similar interests and friends. "We're so close that we know everything about each other. I know his shoe size! I just love him so much." His brother often joins Hector and his friends as they listen to Latin music at home or hang out at a shopping mall several miles from their house.

His sister, who is three years older, often took care of him as they were growing up. She cooked meals, got him ready for school, talked with him about problems that he had, and "taught me about life." When she was 16, his sister had a fight with his parents and ran away. After they refused to let her come home, she got married. Hector still sees her, but as a 20-year-old mother with three children of her own, she has little time for talking.

Hector says that the most frightening parts of his early childhood were the frequent fights between his parents.

> My childhood, it was pretty good, but there were some problems going around. . . . Since I was little, [my father] used to hit my mom. I used to be the witness and I was sad because I couldn't do anything about it. . . . And when I'm not around, my mom, she don't be telling me, but I know that sometimes he will still be hitting her because I see her with bruises or something.

As Hector got older, he began to intervene to protect his mother who, he says, has "always been there for him" whenever he needed help or support. Hector says he wishes his family members could have "more respect for each other because I would like to talk more to them. You know, I would like to talk about problems that I have, but I just can't. And I want that."

Hector says that he had a lot of childhood friends and had hoped that they would stay friends for life. But he was disappointed because "they all left and had kids. They are, like, 16, 17, and 18. So most of the childhood friends I had, they are, like, gone now." Sometimes, he says, he feels sad for no reason when he thinks about how he has few people with whom he can talk. One exception is his friend Lia, who has "been there all the ways for me" since first grade. "I call her my cousin, but she's not really my cousin." Even Ms. Turner understands the special nature of Hector's relationship with Lia. During a class in which she instructed students to quietly work on a family history assignment, she allowed Hector and Lia to talk.

Hector values Lia's advice, especially when they discuss relationships. Lia told him, "You have to respect girls in order for them to like you. You know, not only that, just respect them for who they are."

Hector believes that boys sometimes have to be strong and stand up to peers who treat girls unfairly. He got into a fight at school with one boy who pushed girls around and called them names. Hector says he always tries to treat girls with respect.

Another person in whom Hector confided was his first girlfriend, Anna. He met Anna when she lived on the first floor of his family's house, and they dated for a year and a half.

> She was, like, she understood me. She understood my feelings. She really talked to me. She was always there for me. Not the world's smartest person. She was kind of slow. But otherwise than that, she was a real sweet person.

They saw less of each other after Anna moved to a neighborhood far from his. He initiated the parting after he confronted her about stories he had heard that she was seeing other boys. Anna's brother, who had been his friend, got angry with him and started telling lies—that Hector was a member of a local gang and was saying bad things about a competing gang. When the story got around, the competing gang attacked Hector and his brother.

> We were standing in front of the house, and it was nighttime, and a car came around. They were, like, "Hey, you know, what you all be about?"
>
>   I'm, like, "I don't know, I'm not in a gang."
>
>   But the guy said, "I heard, because I was talking to Stone [Anna's brother]; Stone told me that you were talking 'dis' about him."
>
>   And I was, like, "No, I'm not talking like that."
>
>   And he set down a gun. I was, like, "You're talking off your head. What do you got to bring out the gun for?"
>
>   He's, like, "You're talking." And I'm, like, "I ain't talking, man."
>
>   And I looked at my brother and I went like that [head nod] and he started running. And I ran for the side and he just shot. And it just barely missed me. And we ran through the alleys, like through the alleys, and we went through the back door and up to the attic. We just sat around for hours and hours. I was scared that day!

For a month following this incident, Hector rarely left his house. He talked with gang members individually, and managed to resolve the conflict. However, confrontations with gangs have become a frequent occurrence in Hector's neighborhood. Hector says he has not been pressured to join a gang, but he is often questioned by gang members.

That's, like, everywhere we go. You can't just go out. . . . They just talk to you hard. "What's up? What are you doing here?" We have to give them a reason. We have to tell them, you know, what gang we are from. We are, like, "We're not a gang." Because we are, like, "We are just looking for the party."

The police identify Hector's neighborhood as a major site for turf battles for several Latin gangs. The gangs frequent the large parks in the neighborhood and control much of the drug sales in this area of the city. The police say that gang members in Hector's neighborhood are older and less likely to be violent than younger gangs. Hector says that "the gangs are not as bad as they look. Just don't talk nothing bad about them, and keep your mouth shut about them, and that's it."

The gang violence in the city was an issue in the choice of the public high school that Hector now attends. His parents insisted that he attend his current high school because it had a reputation as a safe school. Students enter the building through metal detectors and are not permitted to leave school grounds during the school day. They must leave all book bags and coats in their lockers, forcing them to plan trips to their lockers carefully so that they have time to get the books and assignments needed for each class. Dances are scheduled during the afternoon instead of the evening, and there are no pep rallies. All students and teachers must be out of the building by 4:00 P.M., so clubs and organizations often meet during the school's first period at 6:37 A.M. Citywide, there were over 100 gang-related deaths last year, and several students were shot or killed in parks in the neighborhoods feeding into the school. However, there is no visible evidence of the gangs' presence in the school, and Hector's parents were impressed that both teachers and students credited the school's dress code and strict closed-campus policies with reducing the violence and crime that previously were prevalent there.

Hector objected, initially, because he wanted to go to a different high school with his friends, and he did not like the rigid policies of the school that his parents chose. It also involved a several-mile trip on two city buses, while the other school was within walking distance. However, after four years at the school, Hector has made new friends in band and in his regular classes, and he now says, "This school is great!" Although he occasionally tests the system by wearing long colored t-shirts that stick out below his mandatory white shirt, he says he supports the dress code as a way to reduce gang identification. His high school has approximately 2,500 students in grades 9 through 12. A large majority of students in his school (about 80%) are of Latino origin, which also helps Hector to feel at home.

Teachers in both his high school and elementary schools have helped Hector to learn how to cope with the difficulties in his life as well as taught him academic skills. His elementary school was located in a crime-filled neighborhood; however, Hector says that it was a "real nice school. It taught me a lot about life, I mean how to defend myself, how to talk to girls, taught me how to read and write." He recalls fondly how his elementary teacher, Mrs. Rosen, always encouraged him to try harder.

> She kept pushing me and pushing me to graduate because I wasn't going to graduate. . . . So she pushed me, and after graduation I thanked her, and I gave her a hug, you know. "Thank you for pushing me, so I graduated from grade school."

Hector looks up to his high school teachers who make learning fun and interesting, like his U.S. history teacher, Mr. Brown. He also admires Mr. Brown because he is willing to talk about the hard times he has personally experienced.

> He is a strong person. He's been through a lot. He's been through 'Nam. He has seen a lot of grief, and he tells me about it. He tells me a lot about it, and I admire him for that.

Hector likes his music teacher, Mr. Annis, because he helps him to understand music and life in new and different ways. While Hector listens primarily to Latin music and rap music outside of school, he enjoys learning about all kinds of music with Mr. Annis.

However, Hector does have conflicts with some teachers. He really dislikes his current art class, which he is taking out of the normal sequence due to his earlier focus on music classes and activities. He says he is not good at drawing and does not like the teacher.

> He thinks he can push me around like a freshman because I'm the only senior there. So he goes for anything. He just thinks that he can push me around; he can't. I got into a couple of arguments with him. I got suspended because of him. And I just don't like that teacher for nothing.

He was suspended after one conflict with his art teacher and complains that the school discipline office is too rigid and imposes penalties for misbehavior that are too severe. Hector's high school grades have gone up and down over the past four years. He failed several courses, and so is a year older than many students in his classes. His parents encourage him to study hard and do well in school, but Hector objects to the way his father often "puts him down."

> He calls me a heurra—a donkey—because my grades are bad. . . . I had an argument with him yesterday. He's, like, . . . "look at these grades! You know, you're not going to go nowhere in life." I was, like, well, grades are just grades. After high school, the grades in college are where I'm going to show you what I'm going to do. He doesn't know about my ideas. He doesn't know what I am going to do.

Hector hopes to win a music scholarship to a state college, where he wants to study accounting. He has not taken any accounting classes, but he says that he has heard that accountants can make a lot of money. His long-range goal is to open a dance club with his best friend in Balsas, Guerrero, Mexico. However, he will not discuss his plans with his father.

Hector's mixed feelings about his father were evident in a family history project that he completed for Ms. Turner's class. She had the students compile photos of several generations of family members and write stories about meaningful family events after interviewing family members—a project that she hoped would make English more meaningful in a school where a majority of tenth graders fail to meet state standards in reading and writing. She displayed the family history albums in her classroom and invited parents to come and see them. She was initially dismayed by the mutilated and soiled notebook in which Hector put his family photos and stories. When she asked him about it, he said, "That is the notebook that my father carried when he was in high school." Hector had clearly talked with both his parents in writing his stories, but Ms. Turner said that initially the only photo of his father was a prison photo taken when he served a short term for petty theft. She convinced him to include a different photo to avoid embarrassing the family, but the parents did not come to view the family history projects.

Hector is now in his final year of high school. If he graduates, he will be the first in his family with a high school degree. His school's overall graduation rate for Latino students is only 58%. However, his English teacher, Ms. Turner, emphasizes that he has the intelligence to graduate and do well in college if he puts his mind to it. On a recent test on Shakespeare, she says that he had the "most lucid interpretation of any kid in the class." Hector has shown a strong commitment to his music, and Mr. Annis has helped several other students earn music scholarships.

But emotional upheaval seems to be a constant part of Hector's life. Two months before the end of the school year, Ms. Turner described a trauma that Hector had just experienced.

> [One day] he was just hanging. You could just tell there was a droop about him that was really unreal. And he came in a class so very late, and he just gave me a look and I knew something really bad had happened. And so, after things got settled in the class, I had him step out in the hall. And he said that the night before, I mean he was in school that day, the night before he and his friend were driving around and his friend was murdered. Some kid shot through the window, missed Hector, and killed his friend. And I started crying out in the hall too. . . . We were out in the hall for 15 minutes. And he was in school that next day; I could not believe it. And I was so proud of him for dragging himself in and knowing how painful it would be, and he didn't tell anybody.

Although the school offers support services for students, Hector says he does not trust the counselors and did not seek help in dealing with this event. He just wanted to be in school where his friends were. A month later, Hector's attendance in Ms. Turner's class slipped again, and she is still not certain that he will graduate. She describes the dilemma faced by teachers who care deeply about their students but who believe that the final responsibility lies with the students.

> Is he going to put everything together to make those steps happen for him? That's what terrifies me most about Hector. He is the kind of kid that you lose your sleep over. You know, totally can lose your sleep over. What is his life going to be like if this doesn't happen for him? And what is it going to be like if it does happen for him too easily? He's going to think that he can smile, and look sad, and kind of slump down, and hunker into his seat, and, "Oh, Ms. Turner, I'm sorry, you know, I forgot to do my homework."

Hector passed Ms. Turner's course, but he failed two others so he did not graduate. He did return to school the following year and still insists that he wants to graduate from high school. However, he was recently suspended for talking back to a teacher and calling her an obscene name. Ms. Turner points out that he often seems to come through at the last minute. So this year may be his final chance to prove himself.

DISCUSSION QUESTIONS

1. Hector has a few close friends, but his peer relationships seem to be somewhat limited. Speculate on the reasons for this apparent lack of

peer relationships. What risks might such social isolation pose for him? How could this school make counseling services more attractive and accessible to students like Hector?

2. Violence has pervaded Hector's life. What does current research show to be the risks associated with growing up in such an environment? What factors might mitigate such risks in Hector's case? Consider both current and future risks for Hector.

3. What ethnic or socioeconomic influences on language development can you see in the transcripts of Hector's conversations? How does culture influence other aspects of his life, such as his emphasis on respect or his relationships with girls and women?

4. What factors presented in Hector's case might be responsible for his ability to resist the peer pressure to join gangs in his neighborhood? Are there additional factors supported by current research that may have contributed to Hector's resistance?

5. Why do you believe Hector went to school the day after his best friend's murder? What did Ms. Turner do that was helpful? What else might she or the school have done to help Hector? What are developmental issues for adolescents related to death and grief that teachers need to consider when their students experience a loss?

APPLYING THEORETICAL PERSPECTIVES

1. Of the developmental theories you have studied thus far, select the one that, in your opinion, best explains Hector's social and emotional development. Support your opinion with information from the case and your course.

2. Despite the violence in Hector's family and neighborhood, he has not become a violent youth. What might Bandura and the social learning theorists say about Hector's development and his choice of role models? What types of social and cognitive skills are important to survival in a violent neighborhood?

See also "Connecting Across Cases" questions 7 and 8, in the Introduction to this book.

CLASS ACTIVITIES

1. In small groups, debate the issue of safety in schools versus the loss of freedom imposed by rules and the impact of those rules on children's development.

2. Examine research on adolescent responses to coping with the death of a loved one and how adults can help them cope with their loss. Using this research, role-play a conversation that Hector and Ms. Turner might have had after his friend was murdered. For your role play, consider how Ms. Turner might have helped Hector deal with the loss of his good friend.

RESEARCH SUGGESTIONS

1. Research post traumatic stress disorder. What events in Hector's life might place him at risk for this disorder? Report back to the class on your findings.

2. The graduation rate for Latino students at Hector's school is only 58%. Conduct research to determine what the national graduation rates for Latino students in public schools are. Also examine whether there are programs that have successfully increased graduation rates for Latino students.

3. Research programs offered by the Office of Juvenile Justice and Delinquency Prevention to control gangs (see online resources below) and present your findings to your class.

READINGS AND RESOURCES

End Abuse Family Violence Prevention Fund at www.endabuse.org

This Web site provides extensive resources on family violence and its impact on children.

U.S. Department of Justice Office for Victims of Crime at www.ojp.gov/ovc/

This Web site provides information about victims of violent crimes and resources for helping persons who have been victimized.

Institute for Intergovernmental Research National Youth Gang Center at www.iir.com/nygc/

Under the auspices of the U.S. Office of Juvenile Justice and Delinquency Prevention, The National Youth Gang Center maintains the body of critical knowledge about youth gangs and effective responses to them.

U.S. Office of Juvenile Justice and Delinquency Prevention Juvenile Mentoring Program (JUMP) at ojjdp.ncjrs.org/jump/index.html

This program supports one-to-one mentoring projects for youth at risk of failing in school, dropping out of school, or becoming involved in delinquent behavior, including gang activity.

Gootman, M. E. (1994). *When a friend dies: A book for teens about grieving and healing.* Minneapolis, MN: Free Spirit Press.

This book addresses grieving issues pertinent to adolescents.

Osofsky, J. D. (1997). The impact of violence on children. *Future of Children, 9*(3), 33–49.

This article describes the frequency of children's exposure to various types of violence and the impact of violence on development. It also examines protective factors for children who are victims of violence.

Tolan, P. H., Gorman-Smith, D., & Henry, D. B. (2003). The developmental ecology of urban males' youth violence. *Developmental Psychology, 39*(2), 274–291.

This article presents a developmental ecological model of how community, neighborhood, peer, and family factors predict youths' involvement in gangs and/or peer violence.

TWELVE

JAIME

Crossing Cultures and Celebrating Life

———◆•◆•◆———

PRIMARY AND SECONDARY ISSUES

Primary Issues:	*Secondary Issues:*
• Identity development	• Immigrant children and families
• Resiliency	• Motivation
• Social skills	• Teenage parenthood
• Social support networks	• Parenting styles
• Bicultural competence	

CASE

Jaime moves with grace through the crowded halls of his high school, pausing to laugh with a friend or clasp hands in greeting. His progress through the hall is slow, but smiles lay in his wake because Jaime seems to elicit good cheer in everyone that he greets. Somehow he connects with each friend in his path as he navigates the 1,200 feet between his fourth- and fifth-period classes in this large urban high school and arrives just seconds after the bell signaling the end of the four-minute interval between classes. He flashes a final smile at the teacher, who is greeting students at the door, and slides into his desk.

Jaime has found his place at this school and is so eager to learn that he has decided to stay one more semester even though he has more than enough credits to graduate. He is taking elective classes, such as journalism and band, to refine his research and writing skills and pursue his love of music. He is also taking Italian, his fourth language after Spanish, English, and French. In the fall he will study computer science at the state college, supported by a scholarship to play percussion in the college's jazz and salsa bands. He dreams of playing for a large city symphony orchestra but plans to study computers to ensure that he has the skills to "better himself" and support his son and fiancée.

Jaime has accomplished much in his 18 years of life, and he is aware of how fortuitous events and caring people have contributed to his successes. He remembers his early childhood in Mexico, growing up in Iguala in the state of Guerrero, as a time of play, warm family relationships, and early education. Family members recall how he loved jumping into the pristine river near his home, fully clothed. The family did not have a lot of money, but Jaime treasures memories of that time, such as when his cousins gave him his first bicycle.

> They had bought me a lot of little things, and being in Mexico and, you know, not having so much money and actually getting a bike, that's amazing. Wow! That's something big! I remember them teaching me how to ride and I couldn't get it. And they would, "Oh, you go like this." And they were teaching me until I finally got it, and I was all excited. That was really a happy moment.

His fondest early memories are of people in his family and town who tried to teach him things. He attended a Lutheran school, starting kindergarten at the age of four, and was a year ahead of his peers in second grade when his family moved to the United States. His parents began to consider moving to the United States after listening to stories told by relatives who returned from the States for visits. There were few jobs in his hometown and his parents wanted their children to have more educational opportunities. Jaime's father died when he was five years old, and about a year later, he and his mother, infant sister, and aunt moved to California. Jaime remembers that the family had no trouble crossing the U.S. border in a van; "they didn't check for papers or anything." Later, they established legal residency, and all family members hope to become U.S. citizens someday.

Initially, they stayed with another aunt who lived next to the elementary school that Jaime would attend. He remembers climbing over the fence in his aunt's yard to see the school. The school officials confronted him and asked what he was doing there. He was scared and confused because he did not understand what they were saying. He tried to explain about his aunt's house, but they did not understand Spanish. He managed to convey that he could not speak English and the school contacted his aunt and mother. They enrolled Jaime in a bilingual program at the school, which he liked because he could "learn English and at the same time learn. I learned English real fast and then I just kept going and going until they put me in regular English class." He began in second grade, continuing the year of studies he had left in Mexico.

Jaime's mother moved the family twice in the next year, first to Texas and finally to a major midwestern city, where 8 of her 12 siblings lived. The family stayed with relatives as Mom tried to find the best location to "make a better living" for her children. Family support was readily available, and his mother was certain that the large city would offer more opportunities for employment.

While Jaime relished the natural beauty of the California countryside, his facility for making friends enabled him to adapt to the new urban setting. He met Amelio, one of his current best friends, in his fourth-grade classroom in this new city.

> He was the very first person I sat next to. He was, like, the first person I talked to and [the teacher] was assigning some math stuff on the board. And I was, like, "Oh no, what are we doing?" So he was, like, the first person [who helped me] and from then we became friends.

Although Amelio is now in the Army, he stops to see Jaime whenever he is in town and they still exchange birthday and Christmas presents. Jaime's ability to form and nurture friendships pervades every period of his life. Even his teachers recognize Jaime's special affinity for getting along with people and "approaching everyone as if they were a friend." Mr. Vincennes, Jaime's journalism teacher, attributes much of Jaime's success at school to his social skills and his willingness to help others. He notes that Jaime usually volunteers to help the students with special needs without being asked, and teachers appreciate his ability to "talk to anybody and . . . get them to feel better about themselves and actually do their work." Mr. Vincennes described how Jaime helped one youth who had been inappropriately placed in his journalism class despite severe learning disabilities.

> Once I knew that [the boy had learning disabilities] I gave the kid things that he could do, and he was fine. And for a good part of the year he would just

quietly do those things. But I was the only person that he would talk to. And then Jaime just took it on himself to start talking to the kid, and now the kid just walks around the room and talks to everybody.

However, while Jaime values friendships, he admits that at times he finds it difficult to find time for everyone. Nowadays the friends he sees most are those who share his interests and activities, such as band.

> I liked it in grammar school because everything was so small, you know, it's like those are the only people you know, and once you get to high school, and you already meet some other friends here, you got this little other side here, and everybody just, like, spreads around. And sometimes you, after you go to high school, you don't forget about your friends, but you don't talk to them as much as you used to.

His time is limited by school, work, and family responsibilities. Jaime stocks shelves at a grocery store in the evenings to earn money for college and to contribute to the support of his six-month-old son. His son lives with his fiancée, Felicia, and her family about five blocks from Jaime's home. Jaime met Felicia when she started working at the grocery store about two and a half years ago. Jaime had always had many close friends who were girls, but with Felicia he felt an immediate "spark." Their relationship grew slowly, but Jaime has vivid memories of their early days.

> I was going on break, and I was just buying two little boxes of chips. And . . . she was bagging for me. And I was, like, "Yeah, I'll take that in double paper and double plastic." That was four huge bags and just for two little bags of chips, as a joke. She just smiled and, you know, it was like the first little spark just hit. . . . After I finished my break, . . . I went back to work and she just, you know, went over and talked to me and she said, oh, you know, "So, what's your name?" and stuff. Okay. And so we met and then she actually gave me her number instead of me getting hers, which was kind of embarrassing. . . . So I called her, like, so, you know, just actually [to get] information, like, what school she's going to and stuff like that. She was, like, oh. And then she told me that she had a boyfriend at the time too. And I was, like, "Oh, okay." I respected that. And then she was just, we just became friends, real good friends. And we were just talking, just chilling, you know, hanging out.
> And then her boyfriend wasn't the right guy for her because he treated her bad, you know. He wouldn't really respect her a lot. So she just got tired of it and broke up with him. And that kind of gave me a little okay. My chance now.

Then one day she asked me to walk her home because it was late at night. . . . so we were just walking and talking and stuff. And that probably would have been the moment that we would have had the first kiss and we got pretty close, but her father came out of the door. I was, like, aww, man. He was, like, "Hey, what's going on here?" Because it was dark outside, too. I was, like, "I was just walking her home." So nothing happened that time. And then another time, like, two weeks later . . . she asked me the same thing, you know, walk me home. But this time we were just talking more, you know, she was telling me about herself. I was saying about myself, how I was in band and the stuff I do in school, a lot of activities. She was showing me pictures of her and her family. She showed me her cats; she has, like, two little kittens that she had to give away because they keep making a mess, tearing up the house. And I was, like, "Oh, they're cute." We were just talking, it was, like, 12 o'clock already. Midnight. And I was, like, "Well, you know, I really have to go home." Because we both came out of work, I remember, and then it was kind of cold outside for July 16th. I was, like, "It's kind of nippy." So I had a sweater and I just gave it to her, you know, just little, cute little things and all. Then just the first kiss, and from there we just kept going and going until the next day. After that night, you know, first kiss, whatever, I thought she just wanted to start things. I was, like, okay, she just wanted to, she didn't want to take it too far. But she actually wanted to take, she was ready to actually get to know me, see how things got on. From there they just kept going and going and up 'til now.

After about a year of dating, Felicia became pregnant. Jaime said that they knew there was a risk of pregnancy, but did not try to prevent it.

Well, we knew it was going to happen, but we really didn't think it would. And we really didn't want it to happen too early, but you know, in a way, we did. Because we knew that it was going to be hard, but we knew that we both could make it. And that kind of, it makes you feel nice inside.

Jaime says they are planning to get married and hope to have the ceremony at a church in Mexico. Although the parents on both sides indicated that they would have preferred if the youth had waited, they have been supportive and assist in caring for Julian. Jaime says that it has been difficult having the responsibility of a son. He has missed some school due to family responsibilities. The time that he devotes to caring for Julian makes his schedule much tighter. However, he enjoys being a father and would not want to change his life. He says that having a baby is a "good thing, you know. A baby brings a lot of warmth into a family and gets them closer."

Some of Jaime's closest confidants have always been family members, in part because extended family members are always around him. He currently lives in a well-kept two-story brick bungalow that his mother and one of Jaime's uncles bought together in a predominantly Polish neighborhood. Jaime, his mother, sister, stepfather, and three-year-old stepbrother live on the first floor and basement of the house, while Jaime's uncle, aunt, and several cousins live on the second floor. The two families share the yard and rooms in the house whenever the need arises. He enjoys the frequent family gatherings that are a major part of their lives. Jaime jokes that "We have a birthday party, like, every two weeks. . . . So it's a party going on or a family meeting all the time!"

He talks frequently with his cousin, Armando, who is trying to turn his own life around through homeschooling after getting into trouble repeatedly at the public school. Armando encourages Jaime and provides practical advice about scheduling his many responsibilities and interests so that he can be successful.

> And he told me "Just wait for the time," because he knows I can make it because he knows I have the potential to learn anything. So he told me, "Yes, you're going to find a job, and just keep going to school because that's the best thing you could do. Anybody can do it. You just go to school and so you can have a better future," which is true.

Despite his numerous friends, Jaime found the transition to high school to be strenuous. The school was large, with over 2,500 students, and the complex physical layout made finding classes challenging. He was also anxious about stories of how upper class students teased the freshmen.

> We were so nervous and all, especially at lunch, you know. Actually, they got to, like, make me sing the school song. . . . they were telling me, "Oh, where's your agenda?" Everybody was, like, seniors and juniors. And I was, like, "I can't remember." So I was, like, "Here, oh, here it is." And they turned to the page. They knew the page and all. So I was all really, really nervous. They were all, like, "So sing the song." I was, like, "Well, I don't know how it goes." I tried to play cool. And they were, like, well, just read it. So I read it. And they were all really happy and got excited. And I didn't understand why until now. Teasing the freshmen, that's the worst thing you could say for the school . . . it was scary, but then after a while . . . you meet a lot of people and then you feel comfortable in the school.

The school has a predominantly Hispanic student body (80%) but also includes about 8% African American students and 6% from Eastern European countries. Spanish, Russian, and Polish are among the 40 different native languages spoken by its students. Jaime enjoys the diversity of the students and also appreciates the safety of his school, which has one of the lowest crime rates for large high schools in the city. The safety of the school was a major factor for both Jaime and his mother in his decision to attend. He travels three miles to get to the school rather than attending another school two blocks from his house. His mother says that the principal impressed her with her emphasis on safety and a challenging curriculum, and the city's open enrollment policies allowed them to choose this school.

Jaime says that his mother's firm but caring approach to parenting and her constant support kept him from getting into trouble. Despite the demands of being a single parent for over five years, she kept a close watch on her children and responded to misbehavior by explaining what they had done wrong and how to do better.

> Anything I needed, she would always be there . . . [When we did something wrong] she wouldn't really, like, punish us to an extreme or whatever, but she, like, taught us . . . I thank her because if it wasn't for her, I probably would have been right now in gangbanging and taking drugs. But I don't do anything. I don't drink, or smoke, or anything like that. So she was a really positive influence for me. She never gave up on me. Every time I did something wrong, she would tell me. So I never really got to do anything really, really bad in my life.

Mom has always spent time with her children in activities that they all enjoy. When he was younger, she would take Jaime to the park and watch football with him. Now they frequently cook together and listen to music. A keen observer of her children, Mom was not surprised by Jaime's musical talent. She recalled how, as a little boy, he would put cans together to create a drum set. When an aunt threw out his cans, he retrieved them from the garbage.

When Jaime was about 12, his mother met and married Renaldo, a metal worker who came to the United States from the same part of Mexico that she did. Several years later, they had a son, who is now a three-year-old brother to Jaime and his sister, Victoria. Jaime enjoys playing with his little brother and often helps his stepfather fix cars. He says that his stepfather "treats us with respect, you know, the same way that we treat him. It works out pretty good.

And so, you know, every time we need help, he'll help us out." Jaime says that
he sometimes feels sad when he thinks about his biological father, who tried
to "spoil him" because he was his first son. He wishes that his father could see
all that he has accomplished and wonders how his life would be different if his
father had lived. However, his mother kept up his father's teaching and guidance that helped him to get where he is today.

Mom emphasizes that children's success depends on the whole family,
especially when that family has emigrated to the United States.

> Everybody out there, like dads and cousins, [should] like push their sons and
> daughters to study, to try to go, like, wherever they can. Like, go reach their
> goals, put high standards, not just do whatever. And the first thing for us who
> come from another place, you have to work harder, like, never to give up, just
> to keep on trying and hopefully things will work out for everybody.

Jaime echoes his mother's values of hard work and discipline in his
descriptions of teachers that he admires. He likes teachers such as his fifth- and
sixth-grade teacher, Mr. Roblas, who was "strict" and maintained order in the
classroom so that the students could study and do their work. Jaime says that
some teachers can maintain order and have fun. But it is most important that
the teacher "understand everything . . . and make sure you got everything
right." He says that he values learning knowledge and skills that he can use to
"have a better life" and likes to share what he knows with others.

Teachers have also helped Jaime to discover and nurture his talents. In
elementary school, the music teacher, Mr. O'Henry, helped Jaime to understand that he had a unique gift.

> He is the person I owe it all to because one day he took a snare drum to our
> class . . . . He usually takes different instruments, but one day he took a little
> drum and he said, "I want to see if anybody can try to do a drum roll." So
> then he wanted volunteers, he was, like, "Does anybody else want to try?"
> Because a girl went before me. So I was, like, "Yes, sure I'll try." So he just
> did the drum roll and I just did it exactly like he did it. And he was, like,
> "Wow, you know, have you ever thought of joining the band?" And I was,
> like, "No, I never thought of it really." I didn't even know we had a band. So
> he was, like, "Okay, just think about it and see if you want to give it a try."
> So I was, like, "Fine, I'll think about it." I was just saying I'll think about it.
> I wasn't really too interested because I was, like, yeah, how would it be, and
> this and that? So he bothered me for, like, a whole week, saying, "Do you
> want to join the band? Do you want to join the band?" So I told my mom,

"I'm thinking about joining the band." And she was, like, "Well, you know, if it's going to help out with your education. You know how I always support you and stuff." So I was, like, "Yeah, okay." So I told the teacher, "Yes, I will join." So, freshman year I had to take either art or music so I first took art, so that later on I could just take music from there on. So from sophomore year I started with beginning band here, and they usually take you to intermediate, but I went straight from beginning to advanced.

His high school band teacher, Mr. Ambris, also helped identify opportunities for Jaime's musical abilities by involving him in the Music Academy. Students in the Music Academy take courses that meet or exceed college requirements and also take part in frequent competitions throughout the city and state. Through the Music Academy, Jaime took part in citywide competitions—in which his high school band earned recognition as superior from professional musicians who served as judges—and played in the public schools' all-city orchestra. Jaime also took part in a mentoring program for musically talented high school students sponsored by a prestigious performing arts center and attended a week-long jazz summer camp with all expenses paid. Mr. Ambris also helped Jaime to obtain the scholarship to attend college in the fall.

Jaime also admires Mr. Ambris's teaching methods, which have helped him appreciate many different types of music and the teamwork essential to a good band. Mr. Ambris sometimes divides the band into sections based on instruments and has them practice and perform separately. Each section must listen to the others and then they perform together with a deeper understanding of how the sounds combine. They also try out different arrangements of instrument sections to see how that influences the sound. Jaime is currently the leader of his section and spends a considerable amount of time helping with the school's Music Academy. He assists his teachers in coordinating the arrangements for the competitions and encourages his fellow students with his ever-optimistic attitude before each contest.

Having a baby has limited the time that Jaime has for outside activities. While music is Jaime's major interest, he has pursued other interests at different times, such as drawing, yoyos, origami, and break dancing. He also enjoys watching movies and analyzing the musical and artistic features of film. He admires the work of Danny Elfman, a musical composer who created compositions for *The Simpsons, Batman, Sleepy Hollow,* and *Ninth Gate.* Jaime plans to study computers because he sees possibilities of combining his love of music and art through designing computer games or computer animation. A current outlet for his creative energies is the design of low rider automobiles. He explained what is involved in creating a low rider and his current work on a low rider bicycle.

> Well, they customize it pretty much, in different styles. They change the whole interior to make it nice and cushy with velour and all different things. You know, you just let your imagination run wild. They put, like, murals on the car, and they'll throw flakes to make it, like, glitter. There are cars that when you look at it, they put the chameleon paint job so that when the car switches to a different angle, it switches colors all over.
>   That's pretty cool. And, you know, you see just all different things. The hydraulics, the engines and everything, all different imaginations that all the people have just to put into their cars to customize it and make it look nice. And when I moved over here, they started making a club also. It's called Low Rider Car Club. And then my cousins who live in this house where I live now, they were in that club also. And they had their cars, and my cousin was making a bike. I was like, yeah, I would like to make a bike now also. So I had a regular bicycle . . . and I changed the seat to make it nice and cushiony and I started putting the steering wheel on it and everything and all different kinds of stuff. Now I have, I'm also going to build a car soon. I'm starting to buy things for it. I'm also going to finish my bike for my son so I'm taking my present down to him.

Always looking for a practical way to apply his creative talents, Jaime points out that customizing is quite expensive. So the skills he is learning in creating low riders might also be a source of income for him.

Both Jaime and his mother admit that many challenges lie ahead for him. He and his girlfriend both want to go to college, but they are already feeling the strain of caring for their son, working, and studying.

> There is a lot of pressure and everything keeps piling up on you. And you just have to keep getting on top because, you know, you got to work hard and try to do your homework. Try to make sure that the baby is okay. Make sure you are not late to work. And then come back and do your homework again. Come back to school and study. Make sure you go home, and, you know, I got to pick up my mom. Do a lot of things. It's, like, my schedule is really, really tight.

Jaime copes by avoiding nonproductive activities such as watching TV. Mom says that he has always been a very calm person, and Jaime does seem to have a capacity to remain calm in the midst of pressure. Sometimes this involves focusing on what is most important and ignoring all else. Jaime's journalism teacher noted that he sometimes forgets to do things he has promised.

> He tends to be out of school a lot because of obligations with his family. If he is in school where he can be reminded about things day to day, if he gets the general reminders that everybody in the class gets, he is fine. He's fine. If he is out of school, he will not call in to check assignments on the voicemail. He will not visit the Web site to check assignments on the Internet. Basically, whatever is the most important thing at the moment is the most important thing.

Jaime's scholarship covers part of his tuition and his mother plans to keep working to help him pay for college, hoping that he will graduate from college with an advanced degree. But she is concerned that they will not be able to cover all expenses.

She also expresses concern about the economic difficulties that Jaime and Felicia will face as they start their young family. A difference in the cultural backgrounds of the two families adds to the complexity.

> She's Puerto Rican and . . . we are Mexican. So she kind of has different ways of doing things. Because for us, we are a real close family. We are always together. And, like, for her, she's not real close to her family. I don't know if it is still because her parents are separated. We don't know, but she is, like, kind of more out there. She's, like, life's going on, and we are, like, more close to family. . . . We, like, really want Jaime not to come home that late, and if he is going to sleep over at someone's house, to call first. But, like, her, she really has no time limit, I guess. And, like, she could go stay to her friend's house, and her parents won't really say nothing.

However, Mom says that "sometimes she likes that [the cultural differences] and my son likes it. So if they put their mind to it, it will happen." She emphasizes that it is up to Jaime and she will support him in whatever he decides.

Jaime also feels tension at times between his Mexican culture and life in the United States. He wants to stay in the United States because "there is a better future for everybody. But I would like to live over there [Mexico] because everything is more calm." He says that in the United States one is always "rushing to make it to work on time, and doing this and this, like your schedule is really tight. There is no time where you can just sit back and look . . . see all the mountains and stuff."

Jaime's family has maintained ties with their Mexican roots. His mother's siblings are working together to build a family home in Mexico near his grandfather's house. Everyone in the family sends money to Mexico to contribute to the building of the house. Jaime has traveled back to Mexico several times with his family and hopes to be able to continue to visit.

Mr. Vincennes, his teacher, noted that many families who come to the United States maintain ties because of their uncertainty about whether their move to the United States is permanent. However, he felt confident that Jaime will do well wherever he settles.

> Jaime is somebody who is going to succeed because he has got intelligence, and he's smart enough to apply that intelligence, but mainly because he has got skills, social skills. He can get to know somebody and know how to ask them for what he needs. So he will get into a job position and he will get to know the boss and learn how to ask that person for the help he needs to be successful in what he does. He will ask that person what they want from him. He is very good at finding out what people want from him.

Right now, Jaime is enthralled by the wonderful complexity of life and eager to sample all that it offers. He is enjoying the journey as well as setting big goals.

> It's really the little things that really make a huge change. . . . The little thing is just your mom telling you, "Hey, go to school. Wake up early. Do your homework." Those little things, you know, that's what keeps me going and what changes your life. You know, you have got to appreciate those little things. You got to appreciate the big things too, you know. But if it wasn't for those little things, everything just wouldn't happen.

DISCUSSION QUESTIONS

1. Jaime has experienced several stressful experiences in his life (loss of his father as well as several relocations and the stress of becoming a teenage parent), but he has still excelled. Based on research described in your text, describe four factors that you believe have contributed to his academic, behavioral, and social successes—in other words, to his resiliency.

2. In what ways do Jaime and his family typify the characteristics of the Mexican American culture as described in your text, and in what ways

are Jaime and his family different? What are the unique challenges faced by children of immigrants?

3. Despite its large size, Jaime feels at home in his high school and is doing well. He has also had good experiences at his other schools. Identify specific actions by his teachers and aspects of his schools that have contributed to the creation of developmentally appropriate learning environments for Jaime and other students.

4. Using the four parenting styles you have studied and what you have learned from the case, compare the parenting style of Jaime's parents to that of Felicia's parents. Based on research describing the characteristics of children of the different styles, speculate as to the effects these styles may have had on Jaime and Felicia and what effects they may have in the future on the couple.

5. Jaime states "a baby brings a lot of warmth into a family." Describe the other effects having a baby might have on a family. Using research and statistics presented in your text, what does the future likely hold for Jaime, Felicia, and their child? What factors specific to this case might affect that "statistical" future?

6. Jaime states that he and Felicia knew there was a risk of pregnancy but did not try to prevent it. What factors may have contributed to this risky behavior on their part?

APPLYING THEORETICAL PERSPECTIVES

1. Identity vs. role confusion is the central crisis of adolescence described by Erikson. According to Erikson, identity is composed of many aspects including vocational, sexual orientation, relationship, interests, political, religious, cultural, and personality. As a result of this developmental stage, Marcia contends that adolescents may experience four statuses of identity. At which status is Jaime with regard to various aspects of his identity as defined by Erikson?

Also see "Connecting Across Cases" questions 7 and 8, in the Introduction to this book.

CLASS ACTIVITIES

1. Using Bronfenbrenner's ecological theory, draw a picture of the many different social systems that have affected Jaime's life. Include people, events, and systems that illustrate the microsystem, mesosystem, exo-system, macrosystem, and chronosystem.

2. Role-play the discussion between Jaime and his mother and stepfather when he told them Felicia was pregnant. Role-play the discussion that Jaime and Felicia may have had to prepare for their talk with their parents.

RESEARCH SUGGESTION

1. In groups or with a partner, research differences between Puerto Rican Americans and Mexican Americans in history, social and economic status, cultural values, and educational achievement and present your findings. Discuss issues that might arise between Felicia and Jaime as a result of these differences.

READINGS AND RESOURCES

National Association for Bilingual Education at www.nabe.org

This Web site provides information about bilingual education and resources for parents seeking high-quality bilingual programs.

U.S. Department of Education Office for English Language Acquisition at www.ed.gov/about/offices/list/oela/index.html

This Web site provides information for youth who are second language learners and their parents and teachers about how to support their academic and social development.

The National Campaign to Prevent Teen Pregnancy at www.teenpregnancy.org

This Web site provides up-to-date information about teenage pregnancy and strategies for preventing teen pregnancy and supporting teenage parents.

Goldenburg, C. (1996). *Latin American immigration and U.S. schools.* Society for Research in Child Development Social Policy Report. Available at www.srcd.org/sprv10n1.pdf

This report provides information about immigration of families from Latin America and how this is affecting U.S. schools.

REFERENCES

———•◦•———

Allen, J. D. (1995, April). *The use of case studies to teach educational psychology: A comparison with traditional instruction.* Paper presented at the conference of the American Educational Research Association, San Francisco, CA.

Block, K. K. (1996). The "case" method in modern educational psychology texts. *Teaching & Teacher Education, 12*(5), 483–500.

Bruner, J. (1990). Culture and human development: A new look. *Human Development, 33,* 344–355.

Carger, C. (1996). *Of borders and dreams: A Mexican-American experience of urban education.* New York: Teachers College Press.

Charlop-Christy, M. H., Carpenter, M., LeBlanc, L. A., & Kellet, K. (2002). Using the Picture Exchange Communication System (PECS) with children with autism: Assessment of PECS acquisition, speech, social-communication and problem behaviors. *Journal of Applied Behavior Analysis, 35,* 213–231.

Corcoran, K. J. (1996). Teaching family concepts through case study. *Family Journal: Counseling and Therapy for Couples and Families, 4*(2), 165–170.

Erikson, E. (1968). *Identity, youth, and crisis.* New York: Norton.

Fine, M., & Weiss, L. (Eds.). (2003). *Silenced voices and extraordinary conversations: Re-imagining schools.* New York: Teachers College Press.

Freud, S. (1963). *The sexual enlightenment of children.* New York: Collier.

Gibson, J. T. (1998). Discussion teaching through case methods. *Education, 118,* 345–348.

Hetherington, E. M., & Parke, R. D. (2003). *Child psychology: A contemporary viewpoint.* New York: McGraw-Hill.

Hutchings, P. (1993). *Using cases to improve college teaching: A guide to more reflective practice.* Washington, DC: The AAHE Teaching Initiative, American Association for Higher Education.

Jessor, R., & Colby, A. (Eds.). (1996). *Ethnography and human development: Context and meaning in social inquiry.* Chicago: University of Chicago Press.

Kleinfeld, J. (1991, April). *Wrestling with the angel: What student teachers learn from writing cases.* Paper presented at the meeting of the American Educational Research Association, Chicago, IL. (ERIC Document Reproduction Service No. ED347123)

Kozol, J. (2000). *Ordinary resurrections: Children in the years of hope.* New York: Crown.

LaFramboise, K. L., & Griffith, P. L. (1997). Using literature cases to examine diversity issues with preservice teachers. *Teaching and Teacher Education, 13*(4), 369–382.

Levin, B. B. (1995). Using the case method in teacher education: The role of discussion and experience in teachers' thinking about cases. *Teaching and Teacher Education, 11*(1), 63–79.

Maslow, A. H. (1970). *Motivation and personality* (2nd ed.). New York: Harper & Row.

Mayo, J. A. (2002). Case-based instruction: A technique for increasing conceptual application in introductory psychology. *Journal of Constructivist Psychology, 15*(1), 665–674.

McManus, J. L. (1986). "Live" case study/journal record in adolescent psychology. *Teaching of Psychology, 15*(1), 65–74.

Merseth, K. K. (1991). *The case for cases in teacher education.* Washington, DC: American Association of Colleges for Teacher Education.

Merseth, K. K. (1994, November 1). *Cases, case methods, and the professional development of educators.* Washington, DC: ERIC Clearinghouse on Teaching and Teacher Education. (ERIC Document Reproduction Service No. ED401272)

Mishler, E. (1996). Missing persons: Recovering developmental stories/histories. In R. Jessor & A. Colby (Eds.), *Ethnography and human development: Context and meaning in social inquiry* (pp. 73–100). Chicago: University of Chicago Press.

Mostert, M. P., & Kauffman, J. M. (1992). Preparing teachers for special and general education through case-based instruction: An analysis of their perceptions, learning, and written cases. *Australasian Journal of Special Education, 16*(2), 40–47.

Roth, M. A. (2000, Summer/Fall). Rural infusion through case method instruction. *Rural Special Education Quarterly, 19*(3/4), 65–73.

Semrau, L. P., & Fitzgerald, G. E. (1995). Interactive case studies in behavioral disorders. *Education and Treatment of Children, 18*(3), 338–349.

Shulman, J. H. (1992). *Case methods in teacher education.* New York: Teachers College Press.

Sudzina, M. R. (1997). Case study as a constructivist pedagogy for teaching educational psychology. *Educational Psychology Review, 9*(2), 199–218.

Sykes, G., & Bird, T. (1993–1994). Teacher education and the case idea. *Review of Research in Education, 18,* 457–521.

Vitz, P. C. (1990). The use of stories in moral development: New psychological reasons for an old educational method. *American Psychologist, 45*(6), 709–720.

Wasserman, S. (1994). *Introduction to case method teaching: A guide to the galaxy.* New York: Teachers College Press.

INDEX

ABOUT THE AUTHORS

Marguerite G. Lodico (Ed.D. and M.Ed. University of Houston, Educational Psychology, and B.A. State University of New York at Stony Brook, History/Secondary Education) is Professor of Educational Psychology at The College of Saint Rose. She has served as Acting Dean of the School of Education and Department Chair of the Department of Educational Psychology. She regularly teaches courses in child psychology, developmental psychology, and educational research. She was honored as the College's "Faculty of the Year" in 1997 and 2003.

Katherine H. Voegtle (Ph.D. and M.A. University of Cincinnati, Cognitive Psychology, and B.S. Northwestern University, Journalism) is Associate Professor of Educational Psychology at The College of Saint Rose. As a research scientist for the American Medical Association, she directed projects aimed at improving adolescent health and wrote policy papers on adolescent maltreatment and school-based sexuality education. She has coauthored several book chapters and journal articles on adolescence. She currently teaches courses in child and adolescent psychology, educational research, and educational psychology.